Ministry of Education & Training
13th Floor, Mowat Block, Queen's Park
Toronto, Ontario M7A 1L2

# How Smart Schools Get and Keep Community Support

Susan Rovezzi Carroll
David Carroll

National Educational Service
Bloomington, Indiana

Copyright © 1994 by National Educational Service
1610 West Third Street
P.O. Box 8
Bloomington, Indiana 47402

All rights reserved, including the right of reproduction
of this book in whole or in part in any form.

Cover design by P. D. Cooper
Photographs by Jean Valette

Printed in the United States of America

Printed on recycled paper

ISBN 1-879639-30-0

# TABLE OF CONTENTS

|  | Page |
|---|---|
| About the Authors | vii |
| Acknowledgments | ix |
| Foreword | xi |
| Introduction | 1 |

Chapter One .................................................. 5
    The Stage Is Set for a New Way of Thinking

Chapter Two .................................................. 23
    Education Has Customers, Too

Chapter Three ................................................ 39
    Doing Your Demographic Homework

Chapter Four ................................................. 49
    Developing Information Bases for Strong Schools

Chapter Five ................................................. 61
    Image Matters (Whether We Like It or Not)

Chapter Six .................................................. 71
    Your Public School Database Is a Marketing Gold Mine

Chapter Seven ................................................ 81
    Using Program Evaluation as a Marketing Tool

Chapter Eight ................................................ 89
    Getting Your Message to the Public
    through Marketing Communications

# Table of Contents (continued)

Chapter Nine . . . . . . . . . . . . . . . . . . . . . . . . . . . . . . . . . . . . . . . 107
    Marketing Communication Strategies

Chapter Ten . . . . . . . . . . . . . . . . . . . . . . . . . . . . . . . . . . . . . . . 125
    Passing a School Referendum:
    A Savvy Mix of Politics and Marketing

Chapter Eleven . . . . . . . . . . . . . . . . . . . . . . . . . . . . . . . . . . . . 143
    Smart Schools Can Meet the Challenges of the Future

Appendix . . . . . . . . . . . . . . . . . . . . . . . . . . . . . . . . . . . . . . . . 145
    Campaign Communications Tools

References and Resources . . . . . . . . . . . . . . . . . . . . . . . . . . . . 153

This book is dedicated to our favorite member
of the Baby Boomlet

**ANNE LENNON CARROLL**
Born December 19, 1981

# ABOUT THE AUTHORS

SUSAN ROVEZZI CARROLL is president of Words+Numbers Research, Inc., which she founded in 1984. The company provides marketing research and strategic information to corporations, professional associations, hospitals, public school systems, private foundations, school-business partnerships, colleges, and universities. In 1993 the firm was chosen by the United States Small Business Administration as one of the four model businesses in Connecticut. Dr. Carroll has won awards for leadership, scholarship, and business.

Susan received her Ph.D. in education from the University of Connecticut in 1981, where she was an associate professor teaching research methodology to graduate students. She has published many articles in peer-reviewed journals and given invited presentations in education, health, and marketing.

DAVID CARROLL received his M.S.W. in planning and community organization from the University of Connecticut in 1977. As vice-president of Words+Numbers Research, Inc., David provides expertise in program evaluation in urban school systems. He has conducted multi-year assessments for dropout prevention and school-to-work initiatives, remedial education, urban violence prevention programs, Chapter 2, juvenile recidivism, and college placement for low-income students. He also provides strategic planning for public school systems. David consults extensively in the area of campaign management and has had numerous successful referenda and election victories.

# ACKNOWLEDGMENTS

The idea for this book was conceived by listening to the marketplace. Many school systems expressed frustration as they faced formidable challenges and experienced diminished public support. Although the accomplishments of public education existed and were growing, this positive message was not being heard in many communities. As a result, the authors searched for marketing strategies from profitable corporations and successful non-profit organizations and adapted them for their unique application to public schools.

The implementation of marketing principles by public schools will help them strategically capture and then retain community support in tough times, without spending precious tax dollars.

In the process of developing this book, Joanne Calafiore was invaluable in the production of this manuscript. Editor Rhonda Rieseberg was the book's guardian angel in preserving the spirit of the manuscript, while reducing its size to a marketable length. Publishers Alan Blankstein and Nancy Shin demonstrated the courage in taking a risk with a new idea; their leadership characterizes NES. The ideas of Philip Kotler, Tom Peters, David Ogilvy, Jeffrey Fox, Peter Drucker, Cynthia Adams, Fran Archambault, Bob Gable, Polly Fitz, and Jack Veiga all shaped the manuscript. To each, a debt of gratitude is extended.

# ATTENTION, READERS!

If your school (or school system) is implementing some of the ideas covered in this book, please write to the authors at

>Words + Numbers Research, Inc.
>P.O. Box 1373
>Torrington, CT 06790

This information may be used in a follow-up book.

# FOREWORD

When it comes to the marketing of education, public school leaders may see the handwriting on the wall, but they think it's intended for someone else.

Susan Rovezzi Carroll and David Carroll have created a persuasive and factual rationale for implementing marketing in our schools: if public education is to survive and thrive in the future, it must begin marketing its successes *now* and it must also adopt a pervasive customer orientation.

The need to implement our authors' advice has never been greater. In 1970 there were 4 million more school-aged children than adults. Today there are 33 million more adults than school-aged children. In some communities, only 20% of the taxpayers have children in school. And the numbers of school supporters keep shrinking.

Our large base of natural supporters (parents) is dwindling, and some of these parents have also become our most vocal and organized critics, attacking school reform or curriculum movements around the country. This increasingly hostile climate for public education is heightened by growing competition from the for-profit privatization movement, charter schools, schools of choice, increased home schooling with Internet-delivered curriculum, and the growing number of private schools.

The good news is that we have seen schools throughout the United States and Canada build great community support systems by focusing on building effective, two-way relationships with their many customers—from students and their parents to business leaders and the elderly. Many of these successful programs follow the blueprint found in these pages. They conduct research on their image and communication efforts with key target audiences, build and test a marketing plan, and then involve every staff member in the marketing effort. The day-to-day commitment of each staff member is the cornerstone of a successful marketing effort. To be effective, marketing has to become a way of life for all school employees, something they consider in all of their activities, not just an extra effort given when a bond issue is placed on the ballot. The smart schools that implemented a marketing program also use program evaluation to market their success or improve their programs.

Significant changes in image and customer support, however, won't occur overnight. It will take time to shrink the "trust gap" between our schools and communities. It will also require the commitment of time and money by boards of education and central office leaders. But by following the blueprint for successful marketing provided in this book, becoming a smart school with great community support is an achievable goal.

The writing on the wall is clear—public education must act to improve its public image and increase customer support. How you respond to this challenge is up to you—learn and apply the strategies within this book and you can transform your school's troubling future into a future of enthusiastic and consistent public support.

> Rich Bagin, ASPR, APR
> Executive Director
> National School Public Relations Association

# INTRODUCTION

Times have changed for public education in America. The familiar, warm climate of enthusiastic, unwavering community support for school systems has turned chilly, and will grow colder as the century's end draws near. Two major catalysts are responsible for this shift in attitude toward public education:

- The age structure of the American population is undergoing dramatic change. In 1970 there were 4 million more school-aged children than adults. Today, there are 33 million more adults than school-aged children. Therefore, fewer adults have children in public schools today, and that number will decrease even more in the next few decades.

  As fewer households include school-aged children, it will be increasingly difficult to ask for tax dollars to support public schools. Those who do not have children in public schools will question the benefits of investing in school systems. They will have other priorities, including paying for their children's college education and their own retirement years.

- The image of public education has declined, while the cost has increased. People's perceptions shape schools' images. The media have contributed to and reinforced the image that public education in our nation is failing. Beginning with coverage of the landmark study *A Nation At Risk* in 1983, many media reports have depicted American education as disappointing and non-competitive with the educational systems of other industrialized nations. Yet, communities are requested to spend more every year to educate each child. In 1977 the average annual cost per child was $3,000; it is estimated that the average cost in 1997 will be $5,000 per child.

Asking Americans to spend tax dollars in support of school systems will be difficult if the perception that the quality of public education is not worth the cost remains pervasive.

Across the United States, public schools already experience the frustration of community resistance. Schools are faced with formidable student-related challenges and the implementation of expensive mandates. Although the accomplishments of many school systems can be documented, communities often remain indifferent to these accomplishments. Sometimes, the public is not even given information about the success of these schools.

A window of opportunity exists, however.

Successful non-profit organizations, such as the Girl Scouts and the United Way, and profitable corporations, such as Disney and L.L. Bean, have learned the secret to capturing and then retaining customer support. They focus on a single strategic objective at all times: *serving their consumers or customers well, time after time, with attention to small, significant details.* This strategy is elementary and inexpensive to implement, yet it pays off in the establishment and maintenance of strong relationships with the groups they serve.

In the 1990s hospitals learned from these non-profits and corporations and began to focus on their customers—the patients and their families. Services were developed, changes implemented, and decisions made from the patients' point of view. The new field of "healthcare marketing" emerged. However, the healthcare industry's reception of the concept of "customer focus" was slow, cautious, and even cynical at first. Many hospitals that focus on the customer have better images and enjoy more community support since the shift in thinking. That change in image is a great return on the simple investment in relationship-building.

This book was created to help public schools focus on *their* customers.

The essence of a customer focus through the use of marketing strategies was conceived and then adapted for unique application to public schools. The implementation of marketing principles by public schools is a strategic way to capture *and then retain* community support in tough times without spending precious tax dollars.

Chapter 1 presents a compelling case for why public schools should plan *now* to build community support for their schools. Next, Chapter 2 discusses who the customer segments are and provides diverse ways that public schools can begin to develop strong bonds with each customer segment.

Chapters 3 and 4 discuss concrete methods to build information bases that can enable schools to better understand and then communicate with important segments of their community. Surveys, focus groups, and demographic studies are described as powerful tools in relationship building with the community. In Chapter 5, the elusive concept of "image" is presented—what it is, how it is shaped, and how it can affect public schools either positively or negatively.

Practical strategies that schools can implement without great expenditures are described point by point in Chapters 6 through 9. Database marketing techniques, program evaluation models, and marketing communications such as advertising, publicity, and personal contact are identified. Each can be used to shape image, build relationships, and secure community support.

Chapter 10 delineates the method to the madness of passing school referenda or budgets; much of the success at the polls hinges on marketing principles. The last chapter, Chapter 11, provides a summary of the text and lists the characteristics of smart schools.

***How Smart Schools Get and Keep Community Support*** will provide public school systems with a fresh and unique approach to building community support. The evolving "smart school" will turn challenges into opportunities, because a new way of thinking with relationship building first will be integrated into everyday school life. ***Smart Schools*** will face the tough years ahead with poise and confidence because of community support.

**CHAPTER 1**

# THE STAGE IS SET FOR A NEW WAY OF THINKING

New taxes for public education? *Vote no!*

This slogan has become common across America. Voter support for public education has dramatically declined since the 1960s as taxpayers, squeezed by rising property taxes and the cost of living, have become increasingly unwilling to pay for something they believe has declined in quality. Even more significant than the perception of quality, however, is the shrinking market of users and the growing market of non-users—many of whom do not see any direct benefit from public education and would rather invest their taxes elsewhere.

Two elements responsible for the cooler climate for public education are (1) the absence of demographic homework in planning and (2) the image of public education as an expensive product that lacks quality. When these elements are considered along with the 20 significant trends affecting public education, it is clear that conducting business as usual for another decade would be a mistake.

These catalysts can be defused and the trend toward a troubling future can be arrested by assimilating marketing strategies into every aspect of public education. Marketing strategies may include publicity, advertising, or community outreach, but the key to future success is that public education embrace all aspects of marketing.

Many school districts have already taken a first step by creating public information departments designed to keep the public informed of school events, issues and achievements. In fact, many administrators realize their role as educational marketers, or "edmarketers," when they interact with the community. These are significant moves toward improving voter support, but they are only a few aspects of a marketing approach. The means to future success includes demographic planning, a pervasive marketing orientation adopted by all staff, and other marketing tools as needed.

## DEMOGRAPHIC PLANNING

To understand how public education has failed to do its demographic homework, we must start with the end of World War II. American parents produced a monumental number of children 9 months after the war ended. High birth rates continued until 1964. The birth rate peaked in 1957 when 4.3 million babies were born—an average of over 11,000 births per day. Members of the cohort group born from 1946 to 1964 are called the Baby Boomers. (See Figure 1-1.) From the beginning, the size of the Baby Boomer cohort placed a strain on public education. In response, thousands of public schools were approved and built. The birth rate slowed significantly by 1965, and the Baby Bust began as the Baby Boom ended. Born between 1965 and 1976, the 43 million members of the Baby Bust led to a steep decline in the number of school-aged children. When the 76 million Boomers began to graduate, they left empty classrooms behind them.

## Figure 1-1. IMPORTANT DEMOGRAPHIC SEGMENTS

**GI GENERATION (born before 1930):** Many experienced the Great Depression and World War II. Representing 14% of the population, this cohort knows the value of a dollar and votes with this in mind.

**DEPRESSION GENERATION (1930-1939):** About 8% of all Americans, many lived during tough times, but now enjoy strong pension plans and social security in their retirement years.

**WAR BABIES (1940-1945):** These Americans (6%) were born during World War II.

**BABY BOOMERS (1946-1964):** The 76 million Baby Boomers account for 30% of all Americans. During the Baby Boom, there were 3.8 children in the average household.

**BABY BUST (1965-1976):** The smaller size of this cohort (17%) led to school closures in the 1980s.

**BABY BOOMLET (1977-perhaps 1995):** These babies of the Baby Boomers are a large 25% of the population and account for the significant increase in school-aged populations today.

(Adapted from *American Demographics*, May 1993, p. 9.)

In the years between 1970 and 1984, approximately 6.2 million fewer school-aged children entered the public school systems, a drop resulting in 12,400 empty elementary schools. Most school boards responded by closing schools and allowing many existing facilities to deteriorate, even though the next likely group after the Baby Bust would be the Baby Boomers' children. Because there were so many Boomers, even two children per family stretched the capacity of the public schools to the limit. Some children now attend school in trailers or portable classrooms, and a substantial number attend schools that are in a run-down condition.

Many local school districts mistakenly thought a second baby boom had begun, even while the number of births per 1000 women aged 15 to 44 was at an all-time low. The apparent baby boom was really a parent boom. So many Boomers were parents that their one or two children created a large increase in the numbers of students.

Today, history is repeating itself as school boards propose new schools to accommodate the surge in students caused by the Boomlet. But demographic data project the following will occur by the year 2000:

- Only 6.6% of the population will be children under 5, a decline from the 11% in 1960.
- There will be approximately 7% more 5- to 17-year-olds.
- High school populations will increase by 16%, while K-8 enrollment will climb only 5%.

School boards should consider such national demographic projections within the context of local data and plan accordingly.

# Public Education Has a Shrinking Market of Supporters

The increasing problem of passing school budgets reflects the dramatic changes in the age structure of our population. In 1984 Samuel Preston reported that voter segment sizes translated into voting power blocs. If you have a high proportion of Boomers and your referendum addresses an issue important to them, it will likely pass. Conversely, if your referendum is of little concern to the elderly and they comprise the bulk of the voters, you will have difficulty no matter how meritorious the proposal.

Public school systems must also consider voting rates of different age groups. People over 60 vote at higher rates than Baby Boomers, and 18- to 35-year-olds have the lowest voting rate.

**A shrinking market of users.** It was easy to get approval for education budgets in the '60s and '70s because most voters had children in the schools. In 1970 there were 4 million more school-aged children than there were adults. In the early 1990s, however, 27- to 46-year-olds outnumbered school-aged children by 33 million.

No matter how many children you see today, however, their numbers don't equal past statistics. In 1970 the 69 million Americans under the age of 18 represented 34% of the population. By 2010, 64 million Americans (21%) will be under 18. There *are* young children in Boomer households. But by the year 2000 the parent cycle will be ending for many Baby Boomers.

**A growing market of non-users.** The "Aging of America" has already begun to have an effect. Older, child-free adults question why they should pay for the public education of other people's children, which can consume most of a town's budget.

The median age will continue to rise. Already, the proportion of middle-aged Americans, those 35 to 54, has increased sharply. By the year 2000, the number of Americans over 50 years old will increase by 18.5%. The median age of the Boomers was 35 in 1990 and will be 45 in 2000 and 55 in 2010. It is particularly important to remember that by the year 2000, one-third of the nation's grandparents with grandchildren under 18 will be Baby Boomers.

**The Grand Ratio.** The ratio of the number of people over 65 to the number of children under 10 years old has been labeled the Grand Ratio by Peter Franchese, publisher of *American Demographics* magazine. In 1950 the Grand Ratio was 1 grandparent for every 2.4 Baby Boomer children—lots of youngsters for grandparents to buy for. The ratio remained high until after 1960, but has been falling since the end of the Baby Boom in 1964.

Today, the Grand Ratio is about 1 to 1.2. By the year 2000 the ratio is projected to be 1 to 1—just one user of public education for every person who has no child in school *and* is over 65. The Grand Ratio can make promoting public education more difficult.

## Trends Affecting Public Education

Each of the trends listed in Figure 1-2 has profound implications for public education and makes the case for using marketing strategies an ever stronger one. Public schools should review these trends regularly. Losing sight of them could affect a school's long-term health, while keeping them in mind could help ensure success. Copy these for anyone who can have an impact on your system. Post them throughout the school.

# Figure 1-2. TRENDS AFFECTING PUBLIC EDUCATION

**Economic:**

1. The U.S. will need a better-educated labor force to increase economic productivity. Education will be viewed as the key to economic growth.

2. The mismatch between the labor force and the competency required by available jobs will grow.

3. Each year, one million students will drop out of school, costing an estimated $240 billion in lost earnings and taxes over their lifetime.

**Social:**

1. Twenty-five percent of all children are born into poverty. Children in single-parent households will face a higher risk of poverty.

2. Most children today will never know a mother who stays at home. By the year 2000 less than 4% of families will consist of a male breadwinner, a female homemaker and 2 children. Because of changing family and work patterns, parents will read to preschoolers an average of 2 minutes a day during the week and 3 minutes a day on weekends.

3. By the year 2000 one-third of the population under 18 will belong to a minority group. The current demographic mix of this group is changing and Hispanics are likely to outnumber African Americans in the 21st century. Population growth will largely depend on immigration.

4. The aging of America will continue as Baby Boomers age, and many Americans will not have children under the age of 18 at home.

**Educational:**

1. The public will demand more involvement in public education, yet have little knowledge about how it should be restructured. Educational bureaucracies and local school boards will lose power as they respond to the reform movements. The educational system will become increasingly fragmented.

2. As vast numbers of school superintendents and principals retire in the coming years, conditions for reform are excellent.

These trends are drawn from the 1990 issues of *The Futurist* and *American Demographics*. They have the following five messages for public education.

**Marketing Message #1:** Although education is seen as the key to economic growth, the goal of achieving an educated workforce will be compromised by students who drop out and by the mismatch between required competencies and labor force qualifications. As communities become increasingly adamant that schools remedy these problems, they may force the restructuring of school systems without a great deal of background knowledge.

*Response:* Schools should share as much knowledge and information as possible so that the community can make sound decisions.

**Marketing Message #2:** The composition of American households with school-aged children will change dramatically. Single-parent households, poorer households, and households with working mothers will become more common.

*Response:* Schools should find better ways to build effective relationships with the community and stimulate involvement in public schools.

**Marketing Message #3:** The number of families with discretionary income to support educational goals for their children will decrease in the 1990s. The have and have-not gap will affect urban schools more than suburban or rural schools. Allocation of state and federal resources will be hotly debated, with competition among schools and among regions.

*Response:* Schools should understand and communicate with their key customer segments to ensure voter support. Schools also need to explore alternative funding, such as corporate sponsorship, for special programs.

**Marketing Message #4:** Population growth will largely depend on immigration and multi-ethnic households (see Table 1-1).

*Response:* Schools will have to teach cultural differences and foster an interest in diversity. Multiculturalism must be integrated into curricula, professional development activities, and school events.

## Table 1-1. THE MULTICULTURAL CLASSROOM OF THE FUTURE

Children Aged 5 to 17 (in thousands)

|  | 1990 | 1995 | 2000 | 1990-2000 % Change |
|---|---|---|---|---|
| African-American | 6,915 | 7,745 | 8,217 | +18.8% |
| White | 31,852 | 33,458 | 33,319 | +4.8% |
| Hispanic | 5,297 | 6,419 | 7,526 | +42.1% |
| Asians and others | 1,639 | 1,881 | 2,083 | +27.1% |
| All children | 45,703 | 49,503 | 51,217 | +12.1% |

(Adapted from Ambry [1989], *Almanac of Consumer Markets*, page 19.)

**Marketing Message #5:** There will be a high turnover rate in educational leadership during the 1990s.

*Response:* Schools should use this opportunity to hire leaders who value the customer, can work with diverse and challenging groups, and take risks to reach goals.

## AN OPPORTUNITY

*A strategy for responding to these five messages could ensure that Baby Boomers become lifelong supporters of public education.* If public education develops strong ties with the Boomers, it will forge an alliance with the largest, most educated, and most influential bloc of supporters to date.

**The parent boom.** The easiest time to forge a lasting alliance with Baby Boomers is right now during their parent boom. About 60% of Boomer households have children between 1 and 18 years old. In a telephone survey of 1000 Boomers, 46% claimed their greatest source of fulfillment was their family, and 44% said it was "work and family." Boomers are the most educated demographic segment in America; 25% of men and 20% of women have college degrees. They value education and want the best education for their children. Because everyday family life for many Boomers includes public education, the Baby Boomer voter bloc will be a significant force at the polls, in the schools, and during school board meetings. This trend is already emerging and will become more pronounced as the year 2000 approaches.

**Empty nesters of tomorrow.** Since these Boomers will be the "empty nesters" of tomorrow, public education should develop a long-term relationship with this powerful group. Such a long-term relationship will help ensure their continued support after their children graduate. This relationship must begin now, however, while many Baby Boomers are parents of school-aged children. After the year 2000 the number of Boomers with children in public schools will begin to decrease. Nevertheless, 1 of every 3 Boomers *will* have grandchildren under the age of 18. These grandparents can be as supportive of education as when they were parents—if their commitment to public education remains strong when they become empty nesters.

# IMAGE
## Public Education Is Perceived to Lack Quality Despite Its Cost

Countless reports have reinforced the image that public education is failing miserably. In 1983 a landmark study entitled *A Nation at Risk* warned of a "rising tide of mediocrity" in American education. After this report was issued, A or B ratings of local schools hit an all-time low of 31%. In 1991 *Time* magazine claimed "the crisis of the common school, the American public school, is that all too commonly it fails to educate. By almost every measure, the nation's schools are mired in mediocrity and most Americans know it."

The public has turned its declining confidence in public education into rejected town budgets and new school construction referenda. Proponents of education are defeated, while education critics are elected. Local taxpayers associations are being formed to serve as watchdogs over school budgets. Such vigilant mistrust takes its toll on those who teach:

> *As an educator, I have felt...like a boxer who staggers into the center of the ring in the final round of the fight. His eyes are swollen, his vision blurred, his body numb and everybody is hollering opinions from the ringside—jab, duck, hook, hop around, get up! The far right thinks education and members of the profession are godless and immoral. The far left think we are too bureaucratic, traditional, and fearful of taking risks, and the middle of the*

roaders have become apathetic, indifferent, and have simply given up. (Mijares, 1993)

While public perception of product quality has declined, the product has become more expensive. Between 1945 and 1975, the percentage of the gross national product spent on kindergarten through college rose from 2% to 7.7%. Although this fell to 6.7% in 1984 due to the declining numbers of school-aged children, expenditures for all schools rose from $119 billion in 1975 to $245 billion in 1984. In 1977 taxpayers spent about $3000 per student; in 1987, $4000; and in 1997 we will spend about $5000 dollars per student.

These tax dollars seem to yield little return on the investment and the public has had difficulty accepting less for more:

> *The cupboard is bare, and taxpayers everywhere are looking around to see where the money has gone. The answer in many cases is that the money has been badly spent.... [There is] a feeling that the pain of taxation has become so great that we must be absolutely convinced that we are paying only for what makes sense.* (Quindlen, 1991)

Yet Xerox Chairman David Kearns has said, "Education is not a priority to compete with the national defense, the trade deficit, the federal budget, drugs, or AIDS. We must think of it as a solution to the rest of the problems." Funding public education may be the most significant investment America can make to resolve domestic problems and secure its competitive future in a global economy.

# MARKETING

## The Marketing Exchange

In its simplest form, marketing is *an exchange in which what you get is seen as more valuable than what you give up*. Think of the marketing exchange as a formula in which $x > y$ ($x$ is what you get, and $y$ is what you give up). For example, Terry usually buys orange juice for $1.99 a carton at the local store. The exchange is orange juice ($x$) for his $1.99 ($y$). Terry sees the orange juice as more valuable than the $1.99 he gives the cashier.

$$\text{Orange juice} > \$1.99$$

This simple exchange can change if the local store is closed on a Sunday when Terry needs orange juice for his sick child. Although he would normally not pay the $2.39 per carton charged by the local convenience mart, Terry decides to pay more for the convenience of buying the juice when he needs it.

Immediate availability + Orange juice > $2.39

However, if the price of orange juice at the local store increases by 30% to $2.59, Terry may decide to spend his money elsewhere.

What has occurred in education is similar to this final scenario. Taxpayers no longer believe the quality of education ($x$) is worth the tax dollar investment ($y$). As a result, public school systems may have difficulty gaining support for the following exchanges:

Teaching excellence > Increase in local taxes<br>
Quality of education > Increase in local/state/federal taxes<br>
New middle school > Increase in local/state taxes

How the school system presents these exchanges will greatly determine whether the community accepts them. One sure way to secure lasting community support is to adopt a marketing orientation.

## The Marketing Orientation

A fuller definition of marketing includes "the analysis, planning, implementation, and control of carefully formulated programs designed to bring about voluntary exchanges of values with target markets [to achieve] organizational objectives" (Kotler, 1975). This definition embodies the comprehensiveness of a *marketing orientation* for a healthy school system. When marketing programs are designed with good management techniques (analysis, planning, implementation, and control), voluntary exchanges of values with key market segments result and organizational goals are met.

Smart schools will carefully determine the value of the exchange and then clearly present it to the market segments involved in the exchange. Townley and Schmieder (1993) stress that

> *if public schools are to remain viable and strong, [they] must gain community support by focusing on students and the benefits of tax supported public education. If the message is not focused on children and the direct benefits to society of public education, public schools as we know them today will disappear.*

*Educators must undertake all analysis, planning, implementation, and control with the marketing exchange in mind.* Educators, like their corporate counterparts, must *market the value* inherent in the exchange. How will the target segment in this exchange benefit from the program, service, budget, school, and/or school systems? What is the value to them? Smart schools will develop every idea with the marketing exchange in mind by asking:

*Is what taxpayers get more valuable than what they must give up?*

The answer must be an unequivocal "yes!" The value of an exchange must then be communicated to the target segments—the customers—who decide whether to accept or reject the proposed exchange.

## EdMarketing May Emerge as a New Discipline

When the Academy of Health Services Marketing held its first national symposium in 1980, attendance was a mere 150. In 1992 the attendance was 600. Even the most optimistic supporters would not have predicted a 300% increase of interest in applying marketing principles to health care. Today, hospital CEOs make marketing a top priority.

To a lesser degree, this scenario will apply to public education in the future, with EdMarketing being valued as highly as health-care marketing. Superintendents will view marketing as the key tool with which to build public support and ensure their schools' survival and growth.

Professionals with an educational marketing background will be in great demand and will be well-paid. Any university or college introducing EdMarketing as a discipline now will capture a new market and create a niche for itself.

## Connecticut Administrators Rate Importance of EdMarketing

To determine the level of interest in EdMarketing and the use of marketing techniques and strategies, public school administrators in Connecticut were asked to complete a descriptive survey. Connecticut was considered ideal, since its teachers have the highest salary in the U.S. The tax base required to support the resulting public education budgets has created a relentless, harsh public outcry against public education's costs, product, and performance.

Eighty of the 200 surveys were completed and returned, yielding a 40% return rate. The sample included all superintendents and assistant superintendents in the state of Connecticut in 1991 (N = 200), who were asked these questions:

1. How important is it for school systems to implement specific marketing strategies and techniques?
2. Which marketing techniques are being implemented and to what degree?
3. Who is responsible for implementing these activities?
4. Has EdMarketing increased in importance since 1980?
5. Will EdMarketing increase in importance into the year 2000?

The survey asked respondents to rate 23 discrete marketing techniques/strategies on a five-point rating scale (5 = very important and 1 = not important) and indicate whether each marketing technique was planned or being implemented. Results documented that 22 of the 23 marketing techniques were viewed as important (see Table 1-2).

## Table 1-2. MARKETING TECHNIQUES FOR CONNECTICUT PUBLIC SCHOOLS

| Rating | Planned or Implemented | 23 Marketing Techniques |
|---|---|---|
| | | *Most Important* |
| 4.7 | 86% | 1. Establish relationship with local media (newspaper, radio, cable TV). |
| 4.4 | 68% | 2. Produce school-wide brochure for community distribution. |
| 4.4 | 73% | 3. Produce school-wide newsletter for community distribution. |
| 4.3 | 75% | 4. Meet with business leaders regularly. |
| 4.3 | 51% | 5. Conduct formal evaluations with hard data on special programs (music, art). |
| 4.3 | 73% | 6. Study demographic trends in local population segments. |
| 4.2 | 38% | 7. Form a formal liaison with taxpayers groups/associations. |
| 4.2 | 61% | 8. Develop a computerized database of parents' names, addresses, phone numbers. |
| 4.2 | 81% | 9. Issue press releases on standardized test scores (SAT, Achievement, Mastery). |
| 4.2 | 45% | 10. Employ formal system to retrieve parental feedback on schools. |
| 4.1 | 61% | 11. Survey needs and expectations of all teachers in school system. |
| 4.1 | 63% | 12. Open all budgetary meetings for public input. |
| 4.0 | 41% | 13. Measure student satisfaction with schools, teachers, curriculum, etc. |
| | | *Moderately Important* |
| 3.9 | 69% | 14. Invite grandparents to schools. |
| 3.9 | 73% | 15. Make school buildings available during summer for programs. |
| 3.8 | 51% | 16. Encourage development of parent PACs (political action committees). |
| 3.6 | 27% | 17. Survey community annually regarding school image. |
| 3.5 | 35% | 18. Develop videotape on special feature, program, or school. |
| 3.4 | 52% | 19. Have school logo, motto, or both. |
| 3.2 | 14% | 20. Conduct voter registration drives for parents of school-aged children. |
| 3.2 | 18% | 21. Have alumni association of school system graduates. |
| | | *Least Important* |
| 2.8 | 28% | 22. Institute speakers bureau (staff/teachers providing public speaking). |
| 2.5 | 11% | 23. Develop school-wide photo file. |

Only one respondent gave a rating of 1 (not important) to developing a school-wide photo file.

Although 21 of the 23 activities were rated to be important, only a handful were either planned or implemented as the percentages in Table 1-2 indicate. The level of planning and implementation of important marketing activities reflects a gap between perceived importance and reality.

**Who leads marketing efforts?** Although inadequate funds and staffing may partially explain why most of the 23 marketing activities were not planned or implemented, some reluctance may result from inexperience with marketing activities. When asked who was responsible for coordinating marketing activities, 78% of respondents indicated they were. Since leadership for marketing should come from the top, this is good. Other respondents, however, cited a wide array of titles, such as director of personnel and guidance counselor, for those responsible for marketing, and few of these positions had a direct link to the field of marketing.

**The future of marketing in public education.** Ninety-six percent of the respondents stated marketing had increased in importance in the last decade, and 92% stated it would increase in importance into the year 2000. None felt that its importance would decrease. Survey findings are best summarized by the following excerpts from responses to the question, "Why will marketing become more important?":

- An increasingly larger proportion of the population does not have children in the school. These voters will not pay higher taxes for school unless they really believe that they are getting their money's worth.

- Accountability in schools is more important, and more open communication and collaboration [are] increasingly in need.

- Parental involvement, business interest, and school effectiveness reports all require more public relations and more accountability. Pressure to meet presidential goals for the year 2000 will have a great influence, as will pressure from the business community.

- Tight budgets require salesmanship of our product.

- Taxpayers expect better results.

We need to explain and sell our schools to get stronger community understanding and support.

[For more information on the survey, contact Words+Numbers Research, 25 Maiden Lane, P.O. Box 1373, Torrington, CT 06790-1373, (203) 489-5639.]

## How Smart Schools Prepare for Five Potential Problems

There will likely be problems with the assimilation of EdMarketing, and some might lead to costly mistakes. However, education can learn from the five common problems experienced by other nonprofits when they adopted a marketing orientation.

**1. The discipline of marketing will be oversimplified and misunderstood.** Many have limited experience with marketing. They may define marketing by its most visible components—advertising and publicity. When someone equates marketing with nothing more than designing a logo or a brochure, however, the concept is being misunderstood. Advertising and publicity are only two of the many components of marketing.

Marketing can be compared to management, which involves planning, budgeting, decision-making, and evaluation. You need each component, working together, to achieve good management. Likewise, the key components of marketing—research, development, promotion, pricing, placement, and assessment—must be integrated for optimal effectiveness. When only one is used, an organization's health can be compromised.

This problem will occur most frequently when decisions are based on what educators *think* is best, rather than on what they know is best based on research into community perceptions and needs. If belief that a school's image needs improvement is not based on community research, distributing an expensive brochure may actually project the wrong image. For want of market research, the school has lost time, money, *and* image.

**2. The marketplace will be viewed narrowly to the exclusion of important segments and overemphasis of others.** Marketing in its truest form focuses *on a heterogeneous collection of customers*—a broad and pervasive market. Educators commonly see only two customer segments—parents and students. There is ignorance of—and even resistance to—the many customers of education. Nevertheless, a customer is any person who has, or could have, an impact on your school system, including students and parents, teachers and staff members, local taxpayers, and business leaders. Smart school systems will consider the needs and desires of their many customers when developing programs and services.

**3. Those assigned to coordinate marketing efforts will lack practical experience.** How many Schools of Education cover marketing in a course, workshop, or even a lecture? What will likely happen in education has already occurred in other nonprofits. Bright, conscientious people will be asked to coordinate marketing plans with little or no training and guidance. They will understand education, but will likely have no experience with marketing research, strategic planning, and public relations.

Some schools may recruit professionals from the business sector—possibly finance, public relations, advertising—to provide marketing leadership. While they offer expertise in public relations or image building, their ignorance of important education concepts may complicate the transition.

**4. Many educators perceive marketing as inappropriate and will give it a cool initial reception.** Because some educators see marketing as a slick way of selling customers what they don't want to buy, they may view those who promote and implement marketing activities with suspicion. Others may disassociate themselves from marketing activities or even be hostile. The change to a marketing orientation will be received as is any potentially challenging change—with uneasiness and concern.

Administrators must convince those who mistrust the idea of marketing that the reality is an honest exchange that is progressive and necessary. One method for overcoming this mistrust is to discuss the admirable qualities of one who uses marketing techniques. A marketer is analytical, assertive, creative, informed, innovative, and optimistic.

**5. Marketing will be seen as the responsibility of one person, department, or division.** Who should be responsible for implementing marketing activities in public schools? Everyone—from the superintendent's office and board of education, to the teaching and professional staff, the support staff, and the cafeteria and custodial staff. Ask Disney employees, and they will tell you that marketing is *everyone's* job. At Disney, everyone from the CEO to those who sweep up after the midday parade has this responsibility. The same is true for education.

## SUMMARY

Although convincing everyone in an educational system that marketing is part of his or her job will be difficult, a marketing orientation can only truly exist when every employee adopts it. The enthusiastic example set by administrators will help convince all employees that the existence of the school system *and their jobs* depends on a successful and pervasive marketing orientation. If employees embrace this concept, their school will gain a customer-driven sensitivity and everyone will be a winner.

CHAPTER 2

# EDUCATION HAS CUSTOMERS, TOO

United States companies have been product-oriented instead of customer-oriented for many years. A product-oriented company develops a product and then offers the customer a chance to buy it, a philosophy embodied best by Henry Ford who once said customers could have any color car as long as it was black. When a company is customer oriented, it asks customers what they want, develops the product according to customer specifications, and then offers the customer a chance to buy it.

To urge customers to buy products, product-driven companies use short-term strategies like improved technology, lower labor costs, regulated inventories, and tight pricing. They achieve profitability in the short term because these strategies attract customers. But these strategies do not develop the strong customer relationships that will ensure customer loyalty. Solid customer relationships based on a customer orientation are like good investments; they reap long-term rewards, generate repeat business, and ensure long-term profitability.

## How Does Customer Orientation Relate to Public Education?

Historically, educators believed that their product was good, it was inherently needed by all, and the public was grateful for it. Generous public funding and general community support reinforced these beliefs. Any failures were attributed to external forces such as low student motivation. Customer input was minimized by the assumption that "we know better." Education was essentially product oriented.

As discussed in Chapter 1, such product orientation has made public education unresponsive to changes in customer demographics and attitudes. Many taxpayers now believe that the price for public education exceeds the value. A quarter of all students—those who drop out—believe the product does not meet their needs. The number of critics is growing.

Public schools must switch from a product- to a customer-centered mentality. Like many American companies, public education has mistakenly relied on inside-outside (product-customer) marketing versus outside-inside (customer-product) marketing (Kotler and Andreason 1991). Kotler describes the resulting situation as a "discrepant market or market disequilibrium," a mismatch or misfit between the customer and product. He warns that public schools must begin to determine the perceptions and attitudes of their customers (administrators, teachers, parents, pupils, and the community).

An adaptation of the L.L. Bean poster (one that hangs prominently in its stores for all employees and customers to see) is a good philosophical reference point for adopting a customer orientation:

## The Customer of Public Education

Who are the customers of public education? They are the most important persons to the school system. They are the students, the parents, all taxpayers, businesses, seniors, professional and non-professional staff, the government, professional associations, accreditors, the media, bus drivers, child care workers, and any other individual or group who has or may have an impact on our school system. These are customers.

The customer is not an interruption of our work. He or she is the purpose of our work. We are not doing customers a favor by offering education as a product for their consumption; they are giving us the opportunity to do so. The customer is not someone to argue with or match wits with. Nobody ever wins an argument with a customer and no one should try to.

A customer is someone who brings us his or her needs and desires. It is our job to care for those needs and desires.

(Adapted with permission of L.L. Bean)

**Characteristics.** Customer-oriented schools create an experience which exceeds customer expectations, solicits complaints, and resolves problems quickly. Important characteristics of a customer-oriented school include the following:

1. Everyone understands the direct relationship between the customer and the school's future.

2. Any investment made to satisfy the customer is seen as an investment in the school's future.

3. The customer is treated with trust and respect. Customer complaints are viewed as opportunities for improvement, not annoyances.

4. All employees are responsible for treating customers well. If you have contact with a customer, you are considered to be a marketer.

5. All employees are trained to have positive customer attitudes. Staff members are trained in the specific do's and don'ts of good customer relations.

6. Customer-driven schools thoroughly, systematically, and periodically evaluate the delivery of a customer orientation. Employees who do a good job at delivering this are rewarded.

**Benefits.** There are enormous benefits to be gained by embracing a customer orientation:

1. Customers will pay more for public education when they feel it provides greater satisfaction for them.

2. Customers will pay more for public education when they feel it is responsive to customer needs and input.

3. A customer focus generates increased community support, which increases long-term health.

4. A customer focus creates new ideas for program/service development because of its emphasis on listening to the customer.

5. A customer focus enables schools to make improvements before they lose customer support.

6. Employees are motivated because they feel they are part of a winning team. Statements like "I'll take care of that for you" or "thank you for telling me that" create a positive relationship with customers that will pay off in loyalty for a long, long time.

## 10 Steps toward Becoming a Customer-oriented School

Switching to a customer orientation requires planning, effort, and commitment. When public schools become customer-centered organizations, they will:

1. Conduct organizational reviews to *determine what barriers exist to a customer focus,* ways to break down the barriers, and methods of constructing a new message spelled "customer."

2. *Identify all contact points with the customer,* assess their impact, and then make as many of them as possible into a positive experience.

3. *Review all policies* to determine if they are made for the school's benefit or the customer's benefit. Examine whether policies are facilitating smooth transactions between the school and the customer.

4. *Have all employees embrace a positive customer attitude.* Clearly establish that a direct relationship exists between the customer and the future of the public school system. There must be a consensus to be more customer-driven at every level in the organization.

5. *Recognize that any investment/effort made to satisfy the customer will benefit the school system.*

6. *Always treat each and every customer segment with respect, trust, intelligence, and courtesy.* Each complaint must be seen as an opportunity to take action, not an occasion to postpone, dismiss, ignore, or avoid the customer.

7. *Train all employees in the do's and don'ts* of customer orientation with the assumption that people will act the "right way" if they are trained properly.

8. *Evaluate all staff and the school system itself* on the implementation of this customer-oriented philosophy. Base rewards on exemplary displays of customer orientation.

9. *Put systematic and thorough input mechanisms in place* so that customers can regularly communicate what they want, need, like, and dislike both informally throughout the year and formally once a year. Review and post these data.окрем
10. *Conduct all strategic planning with the customer's needs and wants in mind.*

## The Major Benefit for Public Schools: Image Building

The presence or absence of a customer-driven philosophy greatly affects a school system's image. Renihan and Renihan (1984) describe image as "the feelings developed by various publics [customers] as a result of their observations and experiences of the school accrued over the long term." In public education, customer experiences and contacts are numerous and cumulative. Because image can significantly affect the successes or failures in public education, it is critical to evaluate the interaction points between your school system and the customer and to evaluate the *overall* customer orientation.

Ron Zemke in *The Service Edge* (1990) called these interactions "moments of truth." Each time a customer meets the principal, speaks with teachers, waits at the front desk, calls the secretary, attends a school event, or delivers or picks up a child or grandchild, there is an opportunity for evaluation—a moment of truth when perceptions are shaped. These little interactions may seem insignificant, but their cumulative effect can make an impression which is tough to shake. If customers have a cumulative memory of good experiences, then they develop a good image of the school and are far more likely to support the school system.

## A Tough Message for Educators to Accept

In *A Passion for Excellence,* Peters and Austin (1985) call customer orientation a "flash of the obvious"—a common-sense approach of doing simple things like

> *answering the phones and otherwise behaving with common courtesy toward the customers. Making things work. Listening to the customers and asking them for their ideas. Then acting on them. Listening to your people and asking them for ideas. Then acting on them. Wandering around with customers, your people, your suppliers. Paying attention to pride, trust, enthusiasm—a passion and love.*

The return on this inexpensive investment of time and effort is enormous for today's public schools. Nevertheless, convincing educators to understand, accept, and implement a customer orientation will be very difficult. It is not impossible, however, particularly if leadership is strong, committed, and unwavering.

Figure 2-1 lists some of the numerous reasons you may hear when people tell you a customer orientation will not work. This list could be posted and pointed to whenever there are objections. A sense of humor should melt some of the resistance and give the effort a little boost.

## Figure 2-1. 15 WAYS TO SAY "NO" TO EDMARKETING

1. We tried that already.
2. No one has time for that.
3. We don't have the staff.
4. Good idea but totally impractical.
5. We've always done it this way.
6. That isn't in my job description.
7. No one wants to do it.
8. Parents won't like it.
9. I don't have the ability.
10. The policy is already in place.
11. That is crazy.
12. People aren't ready for this.
13. The unions will fight you.
14. We don't need it.
15. It won't work here.

# Identifying the Customer Segments of Public Education

If most educators were asked who the customers were in public education, the likely response would be "students." Students directly consume the product so this perception is logical. Some respondents would also include the parents of students.

In reality, the customer—or market—profiles for public education are complex and broad. Each taxpayer is a customer. Other marketing exchanges, however, far exceed a simple monetary exchange. Board of Education members volunteer their time for quality education. The Parent Teacher Organization (PTO) has fundraisers to provide the school with adjunct programming. Teachers provide their expertise and skills for a competitive salary. All are customers of public education. Identifying these customers and determining their levels of interest is critical, and this refinement is achieved through market segmentation.

## Market Segmentation

Dividing customers into many smaller homogeneous clusters creates market segments—smaller groups that share similar characteristics such as age, ethnicity, lifestyle, or political orientation. The ability of a school system to identify and develop a relationship with its market segments will determine the overall success of its customer orientation efforts.

For example, the important market segment of parents can actually comprise many customer segments based on age of the children, voter registration, voting rates, and other key factors that segment the parent group into smaller, homogeneous groups. Such market segmentation should be applied to the many customers of public education, including the internal (school system employees) or external (everyone else) customers listed in Figure 2-2. Each is (or can be) engaged in a marketing exchange with the school system.

## Figure 2-2. POTENTIAL MARKET SEGMENTS

**External**

| | | |
|---|---|---|
| Accreditors | Fire department personnel | PTO/PTA |
| Alumni | Health-care providers | Senior citizens |
| Board of Education | Media personnel | Social services personnel |
| Business persons | Parents | Special interest groups |
| Community leaders | Police department personnel | Students |
| Elected officials | Professional organizations | |

**Internal**

| | | |
|---|---|---|
| Administrators | Other professional staff | Secretarial support staff |
| Teachers | Student personnel | Other nonprofessional staff |

Not all market segments are equally important to a public school system. Parents of current students are more important than parents of alumni, for example. Even so, school systems have viewed their market segments so narrowly in the past that their many exclusions have left them in a precarious and vulnerable position. Relationships with many customer segments, such as senior citizens, have been undeveloped or underdeveloped, leaving their support for schools to chance.

The challenge for the public school is to identify and understand its customer segments and then focus on building relationships with the key market segments. Corey Elementary School in Arlington, Texas, has already discovered the value of this strategy through its 10 programs that link the school with customer segments (Kenner and Gribbin, 1992).

## Customer Orientation in the External Marketplace

### *Parents*

As the primary external customer segment, parents are worthy of significant attention. Their direct use of public education has given them extensive firsthand experience with the school system. Because of these many moments of truth, the school system must make a concerted effort to extend a customer orientation. Unfortunately, because schools tend to passively accept, rather than actively cultivate, their relationship with parents, public schools must strive to overcome three problems.

First, parents often visit school only when requested. Sometimes this reluctance is because the school is perceived as "unwelcoming." Second, public school staff often convey the negative beliefs that parents aren't interested in school, they never show up, they promise but don't follow through, they do homework for children, and they worry too much about what other children are doing. Third, the school may seem like a forbidding fortress, giving the message, "Don't stay too long, if you come at all." Examples include the lack of a sign, the need to make an appointment first, the receptionist's abrupt telephone manner, the lack of adult-sized chairs in classrooms, the unwillingness of staff to be interrupted, and the lack of parking.

How do you create a customer orientation for this key market segment? You can start with a brainstorming session between school faculty and the PTO/PTA to generate ideas, such as those listed below. They are based on three guiding principles: make plans based on family demographics, create more channels for communication, and develop programs that encourage lifelong support.

**1. Plan with the changing demographic nature of the family in mind.** Today, 80% of white children, 38% of African-American children and 67% of Hispanic children live with two parents. Also, 13% of African-American children, compared with 5% of Hispanic and 3% of white children, live with grandparents. These percentages will continue to change.

When scheduling school activities and special events, take the needs of parents into account. Working parents are the norm, more families relocate frequently, many have a first language other than English, and some represent many different cultures.

## Customer Orientation Activities for Parents

- Host a welcome orientation for new families in the community.
- To help working parents, coordinate with child care agencies for snow days, delayed openings, or inservice days to help working parents.

- Provide an after-school program for children whose parents work.
- Designate a room for children who become sick in school and cannot be immediately picked up.
- Provide transportation to school functions.
- Offer day care during evening parent-teacher conferences.
- Have bilingual capabilities.
- Design special events to bring *all* parents into schools.

**2. Create more channels for communication.** Anne Henderson (1986) recommends you keep the school open and friendly by providing faster two-way communication and encouraging parents to comment on policies and even share in decision-making; creating parent-school partnering strategies; and promoting involvement and participation.

Listen to parents. What do they think about school policies, programs, curricula, grading, and other concerns? Put parents on committees, and invite them to your meetings. The annual 10-minute parent-teacher conferences should be a relic of the past.

## Customer Orientation Activities for Parents

- Distribute a school calendar of special events and important school year dates. Include names and phone numbers of any staff member parents may need to contact.
- Write more notes to parents. Research has shown that parents cherish a few lines from a teacher.
- Call students' parents at the beginning of the school year.
- Have open-door classroom visitation.
- Provide "roll-over" telephone lines so parents will not hear a busy signal, and provide an emergency access number to your school.
- Send home updates of student progress on Friday. (One sentence is better than nothing.)
- Hold a parent-teacher luncheon in the cafeteria.
- Meet parents after school hours.

- Ensure the school receptionist knows all school hours, policies, and procedures, and can redirect calls as needed.
- Meet parents in nonschool settings.
- Return all phone calls during the school day.
- Provide translations of written communication for non-English-speaking parents.
- Hold a weekly coffee klatch so parents can chat with staff about concerns.
- Create formal and informal opportunities to collect input from parents (suggestion boxes, focus groups, surveys).

**3. Develop programs that encourage lifelong support of public education.** As the number of parents of school-aged children declines and the number of empty nesters grows, public education must increasingly rely on the parents of alumni for support. Developing a lifelong relationship is significantly easier when parents still have children in school.

## Customer Orientation Activities for Parents of Alumni

- Organize a parent-alumni volunteer program, and encourage teachers to use these volunteers in the classroom.
- Open special events at the school to the parent-alumni group.

Townley and Schmieder (1993) suggest other innovative, inexpensive ways to develop relationships with these key customers. Hines (1993) suggests that special activities include others as well as parents: "Inviting grandparents to school on a special day dedicated to them creates [a] positive feeling in the community. Even community members with no children in the public schools welcome invitations to participate in such simple and inexpensive activities as brown bag concerts."

## *Other External Market Segments*

Customer orientation requires an active relationship between all external market segments and the public school. A school's customers can also become tutors and mentors, assist in music and art, offer internships and workplace tours, and assume many other roles. They can organize voter registration drives and campaign committees.

Schools can develop active relationships by including these individuals in any group where policy and programming are discussed. Begin and end all meetings on time, have an agenda, and stick to it. Always thank volunteers for their contributions.

## Customer Orientation Activities for External Segments

- Review policies, programs, and activities to encourage external market participation and eliminate barriers to a customer orientation.
- Offer the external market active and diverse ways to interact with your school.
- Give the school a welcoming climate by placing a welcome sign at the front door that gives directions to the main office.
- Answer phone calls within three rings in a courteous and accommodating manner.
- Place chairs, coat racks, and magazines in any waiting areas.
- Offer coffee or tea to adult visitors, and healthy snacks to children.
- Greet visitors immediately in a friendly, warm manner. A smile is one of the school's best marketing tools.
- Never be rude, inconsiderate, or disrespectful.
- Return phone calls within the school day.
- Display photos of students and staff in the hallways.
- Keep the facility clean and the school yard maintained.
- Make sure there are parking spaces for visitors.
- Make some school equipment available to the community.
- Offer selected school buildings for community use during the summer and in the evening.

### *Senior Citizens*

Inclusion of older citizens in public education should be a priority for schools. The growing trend of intergenerational education provides a way for older people to visit schools and work with students in a formal, planned way. Schreter (1991) describes several approaches to using older volunteers.

A positive exchange from such involvement occurs at three levels, with benefits to the students, seniors, and schools. Students show improved grades, self-esteem, and social behavior. Seniors report improved skills, higher levels of personal satisfaction, and better attitudes toward children and youth. Finally, schools develop a firm relationship with older community members.

With school budgets being voted down more frequently, the support of seniors in the voting booth is vital. Research has shown that this group will support institutions they understand. Intergenerational projects make good political sense, good educational sense, and just good common sense.

## Customer Orientation in the Internal Marketplace

### *Employees*

Often ignored as a key market segment are those individuals "just down the hall." Ron Jackson (1988) suggests that smart companies who get to their employees "might just manage to get to the rest of the world." Why is this so?

Employees are the biggest image emissaries a service organization has. The way in which employees characterize an organization sets the tone for its public image. According to retired superintendent Robert Purvis (1993), "if the [employees] tell the community that the school system is bad, then it is bad, and it is unlikely that the school board or district administrators will be able to change that perception."

Happy employees are better able to implement customer-orientation principles. Thomas Bonoma, a professor of business at Harvard University, advises us to treat employees like customers because your customers will be treated like employees. The new employee satisfaction magazine, *QUEST*, advises, "If you want your customers to come first, don't put your employees last." Considering the many "moments of truth" employees have with the public, it is absolutely essential to hire, train, and evaluate staff based on their customer orientation.

Teachers should probably be the first internal market segment extensively trained in customer orientation. After all, they have the most frequent contact with students and their families. Teachers answer questions, solve problems, and even mediate confrontations. If experience with a teacher is positive, the story is repeated and a positive image is built. Negative experiences may irreparably damage the school's image.

Adopting an internal customer orientation begins with two key steps: establishing customer orientation as a goal and evaluating job satisfaction regularly.

**1. Establish customer orientation as a goal.** Hire, evaluate, and reward professional and nonprofessional staff members based on their customer orientation.

- Devote professional development time to customer orientation training.
- Ask applicants whether they would send their children to your school system. Those who choose private schools and live in your district send a negative message about your school.
- Hold an orientation for all new staff where the concepts of customer orientation are discussed and promoted.
- Require staff development in human interaction skills, such as oral communication and problem-solving.
- Mandate that professional development activities include information on effective interaction with parents.
- Introduce new staff formally at meetings, through the media, and in newsletters.
- Develop a speakers' bureau of teachers and other staff on topics like study skills, writing, and parenting.
- Reward staff who exhibit an exceptional customer-driven attitude.
- Reward staff who submit ideas for improvement.
- Reward staff for their achievements. A short note from the administrator, a few lines in the school newsletter, a column in the local newspaper, or even a party for them can foster good feelings.

**2. Evaluate job satisfaction regularly.** Internal surveys of employee satisfaction were extremely popular in the 1970s, but were underused in the

1980s. An effort to serve the customer has made the employee's role important again. Corporations and organizations recognize that if you want to know what employees think, you have to ask.

Because all employees can generate a positive image for the school, their level of job satisfaction should be measured at least once a year. Employee attitudes about themselves, their jobs, and their relationships with other school personnel will influence the school's image.

Leslie (1989) urges that "in discovering exactly what it is that matters to teachers and what they need to do a better job, principals will have the tools they need to significantly enhance [their] teachers' satisfaction in their [schools.]" Her school district in Beaverton, Oregon, serves as a model in this area.

One state education association surveys its teachers' satisfaction with school facilities, school maintenance, school safety, supplies and equipment, support staff levels, work assignments, and opportunities for decision-making.

*Be sure to follow evaluation with action.* Respond to employee concerns and share them with administrators. If there are problems, form a task force to identify steps toward resolution. Then re-survey your teachers to determine if any change in satisfaction has occurred.

One of the most dangerous aspects of taking a survey is maintaining the status quo if there is a need to change (Deutsch, 1990). In one survey, the cafeteria was given poor service ratings. Although the problem was acknowledged in a company newsletter, there were no changes. Before the survey, the employees felt that the management did not know how bad the problem was. After the survey, management inaction said to employees, "We really don't care." Along with the decline in morale, these employees are not likely to give such candid feedback again.

Market segmentation should also be applied to the internal market. Different subgroups, such as administrators and teachers, may have different levels of job satisfaction, and ratings among individuals within each subgroup will differ. All data must be considered in your analysis of job satisfaction. Job satisfaction for younger teachers may be different than for 20-year veterans. Seeing the division of opinions within target segments is critical to understanding what makes employees happy. Their diversity must be recognized when you take steps to improve job satisfaction.

Many companies stimulate job satisfaction by investing in employee training programs that make employees feel like part of a family. In fact, a statistically proven relationship exists between the employees' perception that they are treated as valuable human resources and the level of service reported by customers. Disney's Quality Service Seminar offers its masterful training to a variety of corporations. In each case, employees are made to feel as special as the customer so that they will "do unto others what was done unto them."

## SUMMARY

How can school systems resist the simplicity of this chapter's message and the almost negligible expense in implementing customer orientation? Walshak (1991) provides a compelling summary that applies to all market segments:

> *Getting and keeping employees [or parents, senior citizens, etc.] involved in your marketing enterprise depends largely on your ability to enfranchise and empower them. Let them share in your marketing goals. Keep them appraised on how your programs are working.... Be clear about what you need them to do to keep the enterprise moving ahead and what you'll do in return.*

A school can succeed only when it develops and nurtures sensitive, long-term relationships with its external and internal customer segments.

**CHAPTER 3**

# DOING YOUR DEMOGRAPHIC HOMEWORK

One of the assumptions of education is that students will do their homework. Doing the necessary homework prepares them for short-term knowledge acquisition, for careers, and for life. Ironically, many public schools have neglected to do the necessary homework of studying annual demographic information and preparing for changes in market segment size, composition, and location. A community's economy, family size and structure, age, and ethnicity can directly affect school life (Lindle, 1989).

Although demographic homework is neither easy nor fun, its absence in the public school sector has contributed to the diminished support of public education nationwide. As described in Chapter 1, the shrinking market of school-aged children—the Baby Bust—was preceded by the enormous Baby Boomer segment. Reaction to the Baby Bust led to school closures across the country even though demographic studies would have shown public schools that another large swell of school-aged children would emerge with the babies of Boomers, or the Baby Boomlet. Now many schools are either closed or in an inadequate condition, creating a shortage of classroom space. When school administrators call for more classrooms, more space, new or renovated schools, more teachers, etc., the public remembers earlier school closures and wonders why they should accept these contradictory and expensive requests.

## What Is Demography?

Demography may be defined simply as the study of human populations. Three distinctive aspects are examined:

1. The *growth* or *decline in population size,*
2. The *composition* of the population, and
3. The *distribution* of the population.

Additionally, these three areas are *examined at one time and over time* with an effort *to explain why changes are occurring.* Therefore, the more accurate definition of demography is "the description of the current status and of changes over time in the size, composition and distribution of populations, and the development of scientific explanation of these events" (Bogue, 1969).

## The Benefit of Applying Demography to Public Education

You can fully appreciate the tremendous relevance and benefit of using demography in the public school sector when you consider the three aspects of demography and their practical application to public education.

### Aspect #1: Study Market Size by Asking "How Many?"

Studying change in population (or market) size is critical to the health of public schools. By collecting and analyzing school-aged populations over time, the school system *can* prepare for growth or shrinkage and how those changes may affect strategic planning efforts.

Like many organizations, schools are data rich but information poor. With its focus on the question of how many, determining population size is simply a matter of counting, adding numbers, and calculating percentages. These data are already available in the school system, and simply need to be compiled and analyzed.

Schools should ask the following key questions when they undertake demographic homework on size.

### Total School Population Sizes

- How many students do we have in our school this year?
- How many did we have for the last five years?
- What is the change in number, direction of change, and proportion of change?

## Key Subsegment Sizes

- How many students do we have at the elementary, middle, and secondary school levels? (How many did we have for the last five years, and what is the change in number, direction of change, and proportion of change?)

- How many students do we have at each grade level, K-12? (How many did we have for the last five years, and what is the change in number, direction of change, and proportion of change?)

- How many students do we have at each of our schools in the system? (How many did we have for the last five years, and what is the change in number, direction of change, and proportion of change?)

This essential information should be collected, analyzed, disseminated, and discussed as part of an annual review by leaders in the school systems.

**Determine numbers of newborns and in-migrants.** The more sophisticated school systems which already collect demographic data on key subsegment sizes will quickly recognize that these data contribute to part of the picture. The complete demographic picture can only be captured by additional data that are more difficult to aggregate, but are of critical importance: the number of newborns per year and in-migration of new householders. These two variables can have a tremendous effect on public school systems.

Because all school-aged children must go to school, the number of births per year is a good indicator of how many will enter kindergarten in five years. This is probably the best planning data available. The total annual or biannual number of new births can be collected from the local city clerk's or town planner's office or the state's Department of Vital Statistics or Department of Health. The data will be available in aggregated (total) form, not by names of newborn children.

The same process should be applied to in-migrants. Their numbers are usually available from the local town planner's office or the state's Department of Housing. These data can also be collected on an annual basis and analyzed, disseminated, and discussed along with the birthrate data.

**Develop customized databases of key target markets.** If school systems want to excel, they will take the next step and develop customized information for planning and marketing efforts. Why? Instead of finding out that 500 new births occurred in 1992, the school system will have each newborn by name, date of birth, name of parents, and address. The same detailed information can be compiled for in-migrants. Instead of learning that 50 new families moved into town, the school system would know the householders by name and neighborhood. Such customized data on newborns can be purchased from local hospitals or retrieved from local newspapers. This minor investment constitutes the beginning of a gold-nugget database.

This information can be aggregated on a monthly basis in a computer database program and monitored over time. It may also be used to develop a relationship with two key segments of customers—new parents and in-migrants.

New parents, whose children will be part of the school system in five years, could be contacted now to develop an initial relationship. Why not send a note to the new parents? Introduce the school system to them, invite them to special events, and keep them informed.

In-migrants can also be introduced and welcomed to the local public school system. Families who move into the school district should be prime targets for immediate relationship building. Call them. Welcome them. Give them a tour. Introduce them to the staff.

Again, building relationships now will yield many long-term benefits for the school system.

## Aspect #2: Study Market Composition by Asking "Who Are They?"

Demographic information on size represents the baseline for good strategic planning information. A very important adjunct are answers to the question, "Who are they?" Population size provides a number but does not describe the composition of the population.

Schools do not have homogeneous populations. We may count 10,000 students in our school-aged population, but we need information on who the 10,000 are in order to strategically plan ahead for their needs. Market segments within the population can have important differences. If not identified and tracked over time, some of these differences can create as much trouble for the school system as ignoring size can. Market-driven school systems will know who their customers are. The student, a very important customer, deserves to be known as more than a number in aggregate.

Schools should think in "categories" by asking which groups or categories in the school population should be understood. This information has strategic planning and policy implications. Some categories are listed in Figure 3-1.

## Figure 3-1. POSSIBLE STUDENT CATEGORIES

**STUDENT RELATED:**
- Gender
- Ethnicity
- Race
- Age

**HOUSEHOLD RELATED:**
- Number of parents in the home
- Number of siblings
- Number of own children
- After-school arrangements
- Number of parents working outside the home

**SCHOOL RELATED:**
- Special education students
- Athletic participants
- Music participants
- Subsidized lunch participants
- After school transportation participants
- Hot/cold lunch participants
- Number of retentions
- Number of dropouts
- Standardized test scores

A school system may shy away from learning more about its students' lives by citing their right to privacy. In the case of describing "categories" of student populations, the aggregated data (not individual data) are needed. Total numbers and respective percentages should be compiled, not individual student names and their respective backgrounds. Once compiled, these data have numerous useful applications.

**Using school-related data.** If one school in the district serves a disproportionate number of subsidized lunches, this information may alert teachers to the fact that requiring a notebook purchase or fee for a special event could be a financial hardship for many of their students. There is no need to identify students by name. A percentage will make the point. This important information might not be known if all students are viewed homogeneously or if categories are not identified.

**Using student-related data.** A large and growing segment of Asian students moving into an all-Caucasian school district may have implications for cultural development of staff and students. The cafeteria may need to make adjustments. Increased outreach to parents may be needed. Foreign language offerings may also be needed. If this information is not collected by and shared within the school system, avoidable racial conflicts of great proportions might result.

**Using household-related data.** If a large percentage of parents work outside the home, the school may need to organize a latchkey program after school. Evening parent-teacher conferences and office hours for the principal one night a week may also be needed.

If teen pregnancies are increasing, more sex education programs might be needed. It may be necessary to discuss frankly the question of condom use and availability with parents through the PTO. Boys and girls alike might need to learn about parenting and infant care. The school system may need to incorporate a satellite program for unwed mothers.

If the school has a large percentage of single parents, it might need to determine ways to mitigate the burden on single parents' limited time at home, especially if they work. Designating homework time in school for students might be a necessary alternative since many single parents have no time to ensure a child does homework when they also must tend to daycare, supper, bath, and bedtime responsibilities.

**Aspect #3: Study Market Distribution by Asking "Where?"**

Where do school-aged children live? Is there any change in the distribution of where they live? The practical value of monitoring distribution data is significant. If there are several elementary schools in your district and one of its seven neighborhoods has been plagued with crime, an exodus to one of the other six neighborhoods by families means redistribution in your elementary school population. This problem must be addressed if signs of redistribution appear.

The situation is especially serious when racial and ethnic segregation are sharply redistributing school-aged populations. A study of ditribution patterns will alert you to trends that can impact individual schools, your school system, and even your community.

It is particularly important to watch for distribution patterns in school districts with neighborhood schools. Geographic neighborhoods are feeders for different schools. This is especially true at the elementary level, where there may be several schools that have many different segments of students who attend, whereas there may be fewer high schools with broader distributions.

Regional schools also must consider distribution questions since their populations come from different towns and cities. The proportional distribution of each feeder town and city must be established for the regional school system.

## Applying Demography to Other Customer Segments

The most effective way to conduct annual demographic reviews and apply the data to population groups is to evaluate population size, composition, and distribution in the current year and over time. Not only should students, parents, and in-migrants be evaluated, but all other customer segments also merit such evaluation. For example, public schools should evaluate households without school-aged children since they are part of the community. Their support for public education is needed, too, especially since this is a larger, growing segment of many communities. Public schools should ask the following questions when evaluating other customer segments:

- How big is this market segment? Is it growing or shrinking and by how much? What is the pattern of growth or shrinkage over time?

- Who are they? What are the gender, age, ethnic and racial background, median income, political affiliation, voting pattern, and other descriptive variables that profile the market segment(s)?

- Where do they live? Are they in subsidized housing? Do they rent or own a home in our school district? In which neighborhood do they reside?

If public schools do not study demographic data, they take a gamble when presenting new school referenda, discussing school renovations at public meetings, proposing budgets, and conducting any business involving public input. Replace soft hypotheses with hard data on the advocates and opponents of public education, and you will find that information can indeed be powerful.

## Where Do Schools Obtain Demographic Data?

Demographic data can be obtained by turning internal data into information, using external data from secondary sources, and creating customized primary data.

**Turning internal data into information.** Most schools are data rich but information poor, with massive amounts of data that school officials neither compile nor analyze. Make a modest investment of time, however, and apply simple percentages and descriptive statistics such as means, medians, and modes to these data for a five-year period and—*voila!*—your data become information. Someone just has to do the work. For example, how many schools calculate standardized test averages each year and apply a t-test to the scores over a two-year period to determine if there really was significant growth or decline? Very few, yet such information could be vital in planning.

**Using external data from secondary sources.** Data from these sources are "secondary" because they are collected, analyzed, and tabulated from raw data and published only in summary tables or aggregated form. (The raw data from which the summaries were derived are not available.) In addition, secondary data are designed for multiple audiences and will not or cannot suit every user's data needs.

The best source of secondary data is the 1990 census data reports, which are compiled from U.S. census data and indicate demographic information on size, composition, and distribution. You can learn the number of families with children, the age breakdown, income, gender, ethnicity, race, housing unit, educational level, and many other characteristics that profile your school's market segments. Census data are obtained easily from state libraries, census data centers, and government agencies.

Although census data are free and readily available, their value is slightly compromised by the fact that they are only collected every 10 years, and updates are often projected rather than actual. However, this limitation is minor compared to the data's value.

Other secondary data can be obtained from state libraries, university libraries, and organizations such as educational associations, chambers of commerce, nonprofit foundations, and state departments. Reports are either free or available for a nominal fee.

**Creating customized primary data.** Unlike secondary data, primary data are raw data collected, processed, analyzed, and used by the person or organization needing the data. Although primary data are often the best information you can get, this type of data collection should only occur when internal and external data sources do not provide the desired information. Primary data collection requires more time and resources to take an information project from start to finish.

There are times when you absolutely need to create primary data. For example, suppose your school system is trying to project kindergarten enrollment for September. Although you have considered the population projections from the U.S. census, your community has built and sold numerous "starter" homes over the last few years and you feel the census data may underestimate the number of children in kindergarten. Clearly, you need primary data in order to plan for classroom space, equipment, teachers, and other resource needs.

To remedy the information gap, you can conduct a telephone survey asking all new residents about the number and age of children in the home. Now you have your kindergarten data *and* excellent information on other school-aged children that could affect classroom size and on preschool-aged children who will be coming in the future. Finally, your primary data effort may supply you with an astounding aggregate statistic. Of all new in-migrants, 40% have school-aged children. This information would not have been available elsewhere and has strategic planning implications for your school system.

## National Demographic Facts Affecting Public Education

Several important demographic facts are worth highlighting. Include these facts with your own customized/local information to ensure the best strategic planning and policy-making possible.

**Future kindergartners (children under 5).** There will be a 6% decline in the number of children under 5 years old between 1990 and 2000, and the ethnic and racial composition of this segment will change.

Although the number of whites will decline by 5%, African Americans will increase by 1%, Hispanics by 4%, and Asians by 2%. Also, the number of children under 5 will increase in Alaska, Arizona, Florida, Georgia, Hawaii, New Mexico, and Utah. The Midwest, especially Iowa and North Dakota, will experience the greatest decline in the number of children under 5 years old.

**School-aged children (5- to 17-year-olds).** There will be 12% more 5- to 17-year-olds by the year 2000 than in the 1990s. The racial and ethnic composition of this population segment will change, with the number of African American and Hispanic children increasing from 27% to 31%, while the number of white children will fall from 70% to 65%.

Many states will benefit from the growth in this decade, especially Arizona, California, Florida, Georgia, Maryland, Nevada, New Hampshire, New Jersey, and New Mexico. North Dakota and West Virginia will experience losses. The biggest demographic change will be a 16% increase in the public high school population, and the K-8 population will increase 5% from 1990 to 1997.

**Working mothers of school-aged children.** Sixty percent of mothers with children in grades K-8 and 75% of mothers with high schoolers work outside the home. More than half of today's mothers return to work before the child is 1 year old.

**Ethnic minorities.** By the year 2001 over 33% of all children under 18 will belong to an ethnic minority. Many of these children will live in California, Texas, New Jersey, New York, New Mexico, and Illinois.

CHAPTER 4

# DEVELOPING INFORMATION BASES FOR STRONG SCHOOLS

## PSYCHOGRAPHICS COMPLETES YOUR CUSTOMER PROFILES

Demographic profiles of customer market segments are an important piece of the information puzzle for public schools. Another significant piece is called psychographics—customer attitudes, values, lifestyles, and personalities. Although demographics is key to profiling your target market segments, psychographics must also be considered, since individuals in the same demographic group can have very different psychographic profiles.

**Parents.** Consider the parents of students in your elementary school. Demographically, they seem homogeneous, probably sharing similar age categories, household composition, and possibly income stratum. Yet there are psychographic characteristics that make parents different—attitudes, values, lifestyles, and personalities. Schools need to determine these individual characteristics to develop strong relationships with this important segment.

For example, a school may want to determine parental attitudes before implementing a new health education curriculum since not all parents think alike on this topic. Perceptions about special education programs may also differ. Determining such views ahead of time will provide guidance on the level and type of support at budget time. Information on the community's image of the school, the school system, or education can be a powerful tool for any strategic planning initiative.

**Teachers.** Another group sharing one important demographic variable is teachers—they all have the same occupation. But are they alike? Their attitudes about the work environment, career incentives, mainstreaming, and parental involvement will likely differ within the demographic group. Gathering this psychographic data may give smart administrators and boards of education excellent insights for policy and professional development for staff.

**Senior citizens.** Even though senior citizens share the demographic variable of age, there are many key segments within this population. Public schools may need to determine seniors' attitudes toward new school construction before putting the issue up for referendum. Seniors whose grandchildren attend public school may be your biggest allies if you find out what their values are and where they live.

**Liberals.** Sometimes grouping your customers first by psychographic characteristics and then considering demographics can reveal surprising customer segments of support that cut across traditional demographic boundaries.

A study conducted by Chew et al. (1991) indicates that a liberal political orientation can help determine who is likely to support public education. Regardless of age and family status, the liberal is actually the biggest advocate of public education. If you always examine the market segment by demographics first and then by psychographics, you could spend your efforts catering to conservative parents who may not support public education, while ignoring liberal senior citizens who probably would.

*Smart marketing of public schools is tied directly to how much you know about your customers. Don't guess—find out. It all comes down to doing your homework.*

## Conducting Market Research

The discussion begun in Chapter 3 has focused on market research—developing information on your particular market or market segments. This information base enables a public school to better understand and communicate with its market segments, thus improving its position in the marketplace and enhancing its overall strength. Significant information on your market segments can be gathered through market research when five basic rules are followed:

1. **The research objectives should be clearly defined, written down, and formally agreed on.** Everyone should have the same goal. If there are hidden agendas, problems may surface after the information is collected.

2. **The research project should be thoughtfully designed, written, and formally agreed on.** The minute research projects are proposed, everyone becomes an expert on how they should be done. Seek an outside consultant/expert for feedback on the design's strengths and weaknesses. An hour or two of professional consultation will be worth the investment.

3. **The project design should be realistic and achievable.** A design that attempts to answer everyone's questions about everything will result in an unwieldy project that is impossible to complete or that compromises data quality. Projects should be focused and well-defined.

4. **Project data should lead to action.** Conducting research with no practical application wastes time and money and is unfair to those who provide the information. Proper market research provides practical information you can use.

5. **Don't underestimate the public nature of information.** Once collected, the information is available for all to review. Such data taken out of context or misused by those who do not understand (or wish to understand) the data's meaning could permanently damage a school's image.

## Qualitative and Quantitative Research Designs

One of the tenets for conducting good research is that the project goals should determine the research design. This can be difficult to achieve, since many individuals may propose the design they know and then fit the goals and objectives of the project into it.

The first step toward a good research design is to identify the project's goals and objectives. Select the design that will gather information in the most judicious, expedient, cost-effective, and reliable manner.

Of the two basic types of research, the qualitative method relies on words to create research findings, while the quantitative method relies on numbers. Good research will often use both types in one design to corroborate findings or add insights.

For example, a school system wanted to improve the quality of its high school program. Channeling input from graduating seniors through both qualitative *and* quantitative research designs was considered important. First, the high school developed a questionnaire with which seniors rated the high school curriculum, pupil personnel services, sports programs, facilities, and many other factors on a five-point rating scale. (A survey with a questionnaire is an example of a quantitative research design.)

As an important supplement, the administrators and teachers held several focus groups or group interviews with leaders of the senior class to discuss *specifically* where improvements could be focused *and* to brainstorm ideas for new courses or new extra-curricular activities. This is the qualitative aspect.

For this high school both research designs were integral in generating information for strategic planning and decision making. The quantitative aspect documented *what* perceptions existed; the qualitative component delineated *why*.

## Qualitative Methods

**The focus group.** The most widely used qualitative research method for market research, the *focus group* consists of a structured discussion led by a trained moderator with 8 to 12 members of the target market. A well-constructed list of key questions guides the discussion. The purpose of the focus group is to elicit from group members their perceptions on issues that concern the school system.

Because the ability to generalize information from one focus group to the group's market segment is compromised by the small number of participants, consider holding 3 to 4 focus groups, each with 8 to 12 members of the same segment. If these groups provide the same information, you can be more confident in the results.

Group discussion can be videotaped, audiotaped, or recorded manually in order to review the "words" or the data later on. However the discussion is recorded, the final step is to extract the salient themes so the needed information can be gleaned and used.

Although a focus group is qualitative—yielding "softer" data based on words—its value should not be dismissed. Imagine the terrific insights your school could obtain if several focus groups were held with members of the target segments below:

- Working mothers
- Parents of physically-impaired students
- Adolescents who have been retained at least once
- Pediatricians, school nurses
- Honor society students
- High school alumni
- Active senior citizens

**In-depth interviewing.** This qualitative method of collecting data presents guided, open-ended questions to one respondent at a time. Answers are recorded by the individual conducting the interview.

The beauty of this method is that each interview serves as an independent data point, whereas one focus group is one data point due to the group composition. If 12 in-depth interviews are conducted, 12 data points are obtained. If 3 focus groups are conducted, 3 data points are obtained even though 24 to 36 people participated. Also, the respondent in a private interview cannot be influenced by the presence of others, a factor which may compromise the value of focus groups.

If clean and unbiased information is needed, and the information sought may be politically sensitive or controversial, this method is favored. It is, however, more time consuming than leading a focus group. The same person should conduct the interviews, since themes need to be extracted from each interview.

In-depth interviews may be conducted by phone or in person. In-person interviews will require the most time but occasionally provide better information. On the other hand, a phone interview would be appropriate if you wish to ask building principals about the effect of professional development training on their teachers' behavior.

**Field observation.** Anthropologist Margaret Mead popularized ethnography, a qualitative method whereby the researcher collects data primarily through *field observation* and interaction with the subjects. This tool has great value for educators because it is close to reality.

Field observation involves a formal method for collecting the data from observations of subjects. The researcher must know what to look for and what to observe. Notes are recorded and analyzed, and the findings are extracted.

From the marketing perspective, field observation offers a great opportunity to measure the school's level of customer orientation. The researcher attends a special public event as a visitor, records observations, and looks for specific signs of customer orientation.

## Quantitative Methods: The Survey

When quantitative methods are needed to provide market research information, *surveys* are usually chosen. Survey research is "the systematic gathering of information from respondents for the purpose of understanding and/or predicting some aspect of behavior of the population" (Tull and Hawkins, 1984). The key word is "systematic." Because the collected numeric data from surveys must be generalizable to the population you are studying, survey research is designed and conducted in a more rigorous, scientific way than are qualitative methods.

Higher-level research skills are required to conduct a survey. Usually the researcher has to consider sampling strategy, questionnaire design and administration, data collection and analysis, and reporting to lay audiences.

**Sampling strategies.** Although most individuals claim to have a "random" sample, a sample must have two characteristics before it is truly random:

1. Each member of the population must have an equal chance of being selected and
2. Selection of one member must not influence the selection opportunity for another member.

Random sampling can be very challenging from a practical point of view. In fact, many research studies use random samples purchased from companies that only sell random samples. Unless your population is relatively small, choosing a truly random sample may be an overwhelming task. If the population size is manageable, however, the best sampling strategy is random selection.

To achieve random selection, sort your population frame in alphabetical order by last name. Assign identification numbers to each name. Then determine your sample size. (Research texts, such as Issac and Michael's *Handbook of Research and Evaluation*, will help you determine the correct sample size.)

Next, use the table of random numbers located at the end of most research and statistics texts. Close your eyes and randomly land your finger at a point in the table. If you land on 345, that is the first ID number in your sample. Continue down the list of numbers until you reach your targeted number for the random sample. You have successfully drawn a random sample!

The one major benefit of using a random sampling strategy is that *it represents the population.* If you had 45% males and 55% females in your population of 30,000, and used a random sampling strategy, the proportion of males to females will be similar.

Because random selection of large populations is usually a mammoth feat, schools within a large district may need to use "systematic sampling," also known as nth name sampling because the total population to be surveyed is divided by the targeted sample size. This produces an nth number to be used in the sampling.

For example, to survey 500 of the 5000 5- to 17-year-olds in your school system, you would divide 5000 by 500 and get 10, your nth number. Next, create an alphabetized listing of all 5000 children. (Alphabetizing the names ensures a random order.) Put pieces of paper numbered 1 through 10 in a box and draw one out. If it is number 3, start with the third name on your alphabetized listing and then choose every 10th name (13, 23, 33, 43, etc.) to create a survey sample of 500 children.

**Questionnaire design and administration.** A questionnaire is a device for securing answers to questions by using a form that respondents can complete. The art of developing a questionnaire should not be underestimated. In fact, getting outside technical assistance to help you develop a good questionnaire is the first step toward ensuring survey success.

The questionnaire might initially be developed by asking yourself, "Is there an existing tool that I can use or adapt to meet our needs?" An answer may be as close as your library's collection of education journals. Simply use the *Educational Index* to determine what has been published on your topic and then see if there are data collection tools that you can use or learn from.

If not, begin by listing the information you want to obtain and then develop questions to elicit this information. List as many questions as you can and then let an expert review and refine them and develop the final questionnaire. This expert should have a quantitative background since the data you obtain must be aggregated to enable you to draw inferences. A good questionnaire will have several characteristics:

1. It asks only questions that have meaningful answers.
2. It is simple, clear, and to the point. (Ambiguous questions can affect survey reliability.)
3. It is as short as possible.
4. No questions are offensive, and no jargon is used.
5. It is visually appealing and easy to complete.
6. It has been tested on a similar group to resolve any problems.
7. It has closed and open-ended questions requiring either "check-off" responses or handwritten answers.
8. It includes demographic questions at the end for target segmentation of responses (i.e., year of birth, gender).

**Data collection.** Surveys can be conducted through the mail, by phone, in an intact group, or in an individual setting.

One major advantage to a ***mailed survey*** is that it is relatively inexpensive. You mail the survey, cover letter, and return envelope and wait for the returns. The personnel expense is minimal, and the mailed survey affords more privacy and convenience to respondents. The disadvantage is the low return rate of many mailed surveys. When you determine sample size, remember this is the size you must *end up with*. You may need to double or triple the size of the mailing to ensure an adequate return rate.

Although some believe incentives (money, prizes, etc.) stimulate respondents to fill out questionnaires, the biggest predictor for returns is the respondent's educational level and interest in the topic. If you send a questionnaire to the parents of girls whose softball program might be cut, you will probably get a good return rate whether or not you send them a coupon for pizza. If you send the same questionnaire to all community residents, most may toss the questionnaire and keep the coupon.

Better ways to boost return rates would be to send a second mailing or reminder postcard. Use first class postage, and write a hand-signed cover letter explaining why the response is so important.

*Telephone surveys.* The cost of administering questionnaires by telephone translates into human resources, and time costs money. It may take three to four callbacks before you reach some people. Once you reach them, they may participate in the survey if it does not take too long. The major advantage of telephone surveys is speedy results, with collection of raw data in a fraction of the four to six weeks it takes to administer mailed surveys.

*Intact groups.* Probably the best way to get good data quickly is to have a captive audience. If you have a representative sample in one location where they can complete a questionnaire, take advantage of the situation. For example, the opening PTO supper, which usually draws very high attendance of both parents, may be the ideal time to administer a 15-minute survey to determine the parents' support for art, music, and athletics programs. Likewise, an end-of-the-year staff meeting for teachers, administrators, and the professional staff may be a great opportunity to survey staff perceptions on the new curriculum.

*Individual setting.* One-on-one administration of a survey is not recommended since it takes an inordinate amount of time for the researcher who administers and collects the completed surveys. Door-to-door surveying also requires too much time and has the added disadvantage that people do not like to let strangers into their homes.

**Data analysis.** Quantification of responses should be considered when a questionnaire is designed. A numeric coding scheme should be planned *a priori* for the completed questionnaires and applied to a few pilot questionnaires to ensure that it works.

Once the survey is completed, data coding begins and data entry follows. Using a statistical software package (SAS or SPSS) precludes having to write a program for data analysis. When the data are entered, initiate a preliminary run of descriptive statistics to see if there are any errors in data coding or entry. Meticulous attention to this stage is key to getting good information.

The goal of statistical analysis should be practical, useful results. If percentages and means/medians tell the story best, use them. If you need to determine group differences, you may want to use inferential statistics such as t-tests, ANOVAS, and Chi Square analyses.

One caution: In the real world, multivariate techniques such as multiple regression, discriminant function, or cluster analyses have little practical application since they provide little direction for follow-up action.

**Reporting to lay audiences.** Results should be presented in laypersons' terms and should delineate action to be taken. Focus on what the findings mean from a practical, realistic viewpoint and engage the audience's interest by supporting survey findings with numeric tables, anonymous quotes from respondents, and pie or bar charts.

You should also explain how the study was executed. If the data were important and the study needs to be repeated later on, the report should be a model for replicating the study.

## Market Research Helps You Talk to Your Customers

Market research should be seen as an ongoing discussion with your customers, a new brand of TLC, *talking and listening to customers*. This is what public schools must do more of to regain and maintain public support. If customers really matter, then talking and listening to them will be a normal activity in public schools. These discussions will be held with supportive *and* adversarial special-interest groups (Kudlacek, 1989).

The research study detailed in Chapter 1 revealed that schools use survey research less often than 22 other marketing activities. This may be due to the lack of internal experience or the political nature of customer feedback. You ask, you hear, and then you are obligated to respond. This takes courage, conviction, and commitment. It requires a healthy dose of risk-taking.

Nevertheless, the success of public education largely depends on how well you practice TLC with all of your customers—students and parents, seniors and business people, and any others who have an impact on your school system. Market-driven schools talk to their customers informally and formally through market research using methods described in this chapter to elicit specific information. Schools can exhibit TLC by:

## Conducting surveys to find out:

What middle school children think about the value of their courses.

What the level of job satisfaction is among nonprofessionals.

What teachers perceive as career incentives.

What the school's image is in the community.

What businesses need from high school graduates.

What parents think of English as a Second Language (ESL) programs.

## Conducting focus groups to find out:

What regular education teachers think of mainstreaming.

Why dropouts dropped out.

What parents of disabled students need help with.

Why many adolescent girls have self-esteem problems.

What administrators need from business leaders.

Why many taxpayers feel new schools are a frill.

What high school alumni liked about their education.

## Conducting field observations to find out:

Why girls get less attention than boys in the classroom.

What elementary children like to do at recess.

How secretaries interact with the public.

What senior citizens do, day to day.

## Conducting in-depth interviews to find out:

What bus drivers like and dislike about their job.

What suppliers think of your school.

What government agencies think of your school.

Gathering such information can be as simple as informally asking someone what he or she thinks on the spur of the moment. This informal feedback is a sign of customer orientation.

Providing TLC will become easier with practice. If you are sincerely interested in the customer, you must practice TLC to ensure needed changes are made and relationships are improved. Genuine TLC will create a long-time friendship between the school and its customers. As Henderson (1990) stresses,

> *A school system can't move forward unless it enjoys community support. You can't provide for the educational needs of your students without a sufficient tax base. And you won't get the tax support you need until everyone in your community understands your schools.*

**CHAPTER 5**

# IMAGE MATTERS (WHETHER WE LIKE IT OR NOT)

What we think, believe, and feel towards something constitutes its image, even though that image may not match reality. One corporation may accumulate as much hazardous waste as another, but is perceived to be safer because of its image as an environmentally safe business. Image says "different and better" even though reality says "the same."

Many marketing experts feel that image is more important than reality because image—the sum of perceptions, attitudes, beliefs, ideas, and feelings held about an object—makes people act in certain ways and shapes attitudes towards a product, service, business, corporation, organization, or public school system. To many, the image based on what they see, touch, hear, feel, believe, and think is real.

Because of this, a good image is of utmost importance to the health and growth of the public school system. As Carey (1993) points out, "like a pebble dropped into a pond your public image can have an impact on your own career, your community, and ultimately public education as the ripples of your influence extend to parents, citizens and taxpayers."

Renihan and Renihan (1984) identify the image of public schools as "the feelings developed by various publics as a result of their observations and experiences of the school accrued over the long term." Whether perceptions or beliefs about a school system are deserved or undeserved, positive or negative, they can account for much of what happens inside the voter booth when budgets or referenda are on the ballot. This is exactly what has occurred in public education today. Its image has eroded at a time when the quality of public education is actually on a crest (Mobley 1993).

## How Is Your Image Shaped?

A public school's image is largely shaped by how that school system *appears* to the public. The public can observe *objective* characteristics like the number of luxury cars in the parking lot and conclude that teachers are overpaid. On the other hand, the image of student services might vary depending on the diverse, *subjective* experiences of the public with these services.

Remember that image matters. Schools must make every effort to project a strong image, and such efforts come naturally with a customer orientation. Chapter 2 underscored the importance of exhibiting a customer orientation because the many interactions with the customer—those "moments of truth"—affect image to a greater extent than any brochure, videotape, or public relations effort.

School administrators should also pay attention to the following factors, which can elevate or destroy a school's image:

- Newspaper articles
- Any publications distributed from the school
- Radio and TV reports
- Condition of the physical plant, the grounds, bulletin boards, offices, classrooms, cafeterias
- Curriculum design
- Standardized test scores, especially the SAT
- Colleges where seniors are accepted
- Dropout rates/teen pregnancy rates
- Student/staff drug and alcohol usage
- Athletics program
- Special facilities and equipment (swimming pool, computer hardware and software)
- School-business partnerships
- Student and staff volunteerism in community
- Teaching and administrative staff outreach, service to community

Although the physical plant is a seemingly minor factor, its appearance can significantly affect image. Your school system should visually reflect the quality and care inside each classroom. In *A Passion for Excellence,* Peters and Austin (1985) stress that close attention to symbolic details reinforces image.

Tending to these details may include proofreading for typos or misspellings so that all printed materials will reflect the accuracy expected of students. Clean walls, painted and free of graffiti; floors shined and litter free; windows clean and clear; and a well-tended campus all create an image for someone who may never have had a child in your school or have spoken to a school employee.

## Why Assessing Image Is So Important to Public Schools

Public schools are realizing that solid community relationships are critical to the school's growth and health. One of the first steps in developing good relationships is finding out what image the public school system has in the community. This baseline information then serves as a foundation for strategic planning to change the image as needed.

Assessing image benefits a public school in several ways. First, it requires a school to do its homework and systematically identify community perceptions. Fact replaces speculation, and planning can be based on solid information rather than on the guesses of a few. Second, it will help build better community relationships by telling the customers that their opinions are important.

Additional benefits of assessing image include the following:

1. The information reduces surprises by keeping school administrators, Boards of Education, and staff "in touch" with the beliefs of key market segments.
2. It helps build a strong communication network between the public school system and the community.
3. It mitigates the prevalent anxiety in public schools on the passage of proposed budgets.
4. It provides feedback in a systematic, objective manner.

5. It develops a base for a strong communications system (media, public relations, promotion).

6. It provides a focus on long-term improvement and well-being of a school system rather than short-term passage of referenda or budgets.

7. It monitors change in image over time. (Image assessment should be repeated periodically.)

A school's image can be improved and maintained with effort. School systems that do not measure their image could jeopardize their future and force administrators, teachers, and Boards of Education to constantly justify and defend their goals. The resulting relationship with the community becomes weaker and more strained over time.

Customer-oriented organizations have a keen interest in knowing, not guessing, how their customers feel about them. Hospitals, charitable groups, social and political organizations, and other nonprofit entities that recognize their customers will assess and reassess their image. Customer-oriented public school systems will follow suit.

## Conducting an Image Assessment

The sample. When a school system wants to assess its image, the first question is—who shall we ask? The answer is, all customers, especially your key target market segment—parents of school-aged children.

For a school system trying this marketing activity for the first time, a simple image assessment is suggested. Novices (and those with limited resources) may wish to select and assess target segments, rather than attempt a random sample of the entire community. When you start small and build an inverse pyramid of information, the image assessment data you accumulate will be focused and clear. In addition, any generalizations drawn from the results will have more validity because the sample will be homogeneous.

Once a school system gains more marketing experience, a full-scale community image assessment should be undertaken. These data are the base or bottom layer of the information pyramid.

The following sampling design addresses key target segments in an incremental way by starting with those who use public education and then dividing them into segments according to education level. Assess one level at a time. Then, as the pyramid takes shape, also assess the non-users.

### Users of Public Education

Parents of elementary school students

Parents of middle school students

Parents of secondary school students

Teachers/staff of elementary school students

Teachers/staff of middle school students

Teachers/staff of secondary school students

### Non-Users

Parents of preschoolers

Business community and other leaders

Senior citizens

High school alumni

Parents of alumni

Newlyweds

**The design and data collection tool.** The methods described in Chapter 4 can be used to collect data on image.

What should be assessed? As a preliminary step, the school may ask a representative group of respondents to rate perceptions. The following aspects remain constant and can form the basis of an image assessment tool:

- Perception of U.S. public schools
- Perception of the local public school system
- Perception of curriculum
- Perception of elementary, middle, and secondary schools
- Perception of teaching staff, administration, Board of Education
- Perception of facilities
- Perception of extracurricular, special, and athletic events
- Perception of a neighboring public school system in a nearby town or district

- Attitude toward specific items in the budget
- Attitude toward budget increases/cuts and specific items

- Level of knowledge about local public education
- Level of interest in local public education
- Level of involvement in local public education

- Perceived strengths of the local and neighboring public schools within key target segments

- Perceived areas where change, development, or improvements are needed

- Degree to which the target segments feel informed about public education in the U.S. and locally

A measurement technique especially favored in image assessments is the Semantic Differential (Osgood, Suci and Tannenbaum, 1957). This simple tool gives the respondent several sets of bipolar adjective scales. Between each set is a series of spaces where the respondent can check where he or she perceives the school to be best described.

The simple example presented below shows a public school system that has an outstanding image at the elementary level, but not at the secondary. This finding underlines the need to divide data by target market segments. If this hypothetical public school were assessed as a whole entity, it would receive a satisfactory image rating, but the problem with its secondary school image would be masked.

*Image Matters (Whether We Like It or Not)*

## Semantic Differential Results
# LITTLE TOWN ELEMENTARY SCHOOL

| | | | | | | | |
|---|---|---|---|---|---|---|---|
| Modern | __ | X | __ | __ | __ | __ | Deteriorated |
| State of the Art | __ | X | __ | __ | __ | __ | Antiquated |
| Competitive | X | __ | __ | __ | __ | __ | Laggard |
| Excellent | X | __ | __ | __ | __ | __ | Mediocre |
| Pride | X | __ | __ | __ | __ | __ | Embarrassment |
| Strong | X | __ | __ | __ | __ | __ | Weak |

# LITTLE TOWN HIGH SCHOOL

| | | | | | | | |
|---|---|---|---|---|---|---|---|
| Modern | __ | __ | __ | __ | X | __ | Deteriorated |
| State of the Art | __ | __ | __ | __ | __ | X | Antiquated |
| Competitive | __ | __ | __ | __ | __ | X | Laggard |
| Excellent | __ | __ | __ | __ | __ | X | Mediocre |
| Pride | __ | __ | __ | __ | X | __ | Embarrassment |
| Strong | __ | __ | __ | __ | X | __ | Weak |

Someone skilled in research design and instrumentation should help design and develop the image assessment tool. This investment of professional time will pay off in both the quality and quantity of data. Also, the political nature of the requested data may demand review by an outside research firm to assure confidentiality and frankness. Having an internal staff member design, conduct, and analyze image assessment data may lead to a disappointing response rate, produce calculated comments, and encourage suspicion of results and their use.

## Image Must be Measured Once, Twice...Annually

A public school with a marketing orientation will consider image assessment integral to any planning effort and will see customers as the starting point for thinking and planning. Therefore, one of the biggest priorities is determining image by measuring customer needs, perceptions, beliefs, attitudes, desires, and demands. This should be done every one or two years.

An image assessment should be conducted regularly to ensure that factors contributing to a poor image can be responded to promptly. Left alone, some factors can become costly image problems requiring complex and difficult remedies. The best strategy is to keep your finger on the pulse of the community's perceptions. Get a report card on how you are doing on a regular, periodic basis. If there are problems, try to rectify them and then conduct a follow-up image assessment to determine if the image has improved.

## A Note on Positioning

In some marketing literature, "positioning" and image are discussed together, since they are very closely aligned in theory. The word was coined in 1972 by two advertising executives, Trout and Ries, in *Positioning: The Battle for Your Mind*.

Positioning is finding a position in the "mind" of the market for your product or service, a crucial activity when there are many competitors. In the soft drink industry, for example, 7-Up has been positioned as the "Uncola" in hopes that when the thirsty market wants a noncola soft drink, it will reach for 7-Up.

Today's public school systems would certainly benefit by positioning themselves more effectively, given the negative press they have received. If your school has a model Advanced Placement (AP) program, try to position your school in the minds of your customers as the school offering the best in AP. Determine what makes your school different and better and then use a positioning strategy to create a niche in the market and improve your school's image.

## Changing Your Image

Making the public aware of a school system's positive attributes may improve image over time. For example, if the public believes teachers are lazy, information on the teaching staff's responsibilities before and after school, their volunteer activities in the community, or their students' scholastic achievements may need to be spotlighted.

Patience is essential. Such change does not occur overnight. After the public school has assessed its image, it must plan and then execute initiatives to improve its image. These actions and supporting data must be communicated to the target market through a marketing communications program (as described in Chapter 8). A follow-up image assessment will provide feedback on how well the program has worked.

Schools that monitor their image and constantly work toward improving it have several significant advantages:

1. They are likely to be more effective in securing community support for school projects and instituting changes sought by teachers, administrators, and boards of education.
2. "Them-us" attitudes are minimized.
3. They experience increased parental support and involvement.
4. They have greater staff morale, since the staff feels it is part of a winning team.

The biggest advantage is that once your school system achieves a positive public image, it can be self-perpetuating. This is a major benefit for public education in today's tough times and in the challenging future.

CHAPTER 6

# YOUR PUBLIC SCHOOL DATABASE IS A MARKETING GOLD MINE

A while ago, I received a letter from Joanne Woodward. Although Ms. Woodward probably did not care whether I read the letter, the nonprofit organization conducting the mailing cared a great deal. This personalized letter from a well-respected, high-profile celebrity was a solicitation for funding from an organization I was aware of but had never contributed to. So what was the point?

This organization's strategy was simple but effective. To increase the number of contributors in a cost-effective manner, they determined who their best *current* contributors were in terms of demographic likenesses and other factors and then they purchased a list of *potential* contributors (prospects) who were similar to their best customers' common traits. I had apparently matched their "best customer" profile. The nonprofit organization conducted a mailing to these prospects, figuring that they were the most likely to become excellent contributors. This approach allowed the organization to minimize risk and maximize marketing dollars.

## The Fragmentation of American Markets

This targeted approach is called database marketing—one of the hottest marketing strategies today. It is considered so effective that some compare it to television's effect on marketing in the 1950s.

Database marketing has become so important because the market has become increasingly complex. Try to describe the typical American household and you will find great diversity. By the year 2000 only 4% of American households will be composed of a father working outside the home, a mother working inside the home, and two children. A recent demographic study of teenagers identified 10 different segments. The affluent market in America also has a similar number of subgroups.

In his masterpiece, *Future Shock,* Alvin Toffler was one of the first to identify the great fragmentation of America into numerous market segments. "Shotgunning," or using one marketing message/strategy for all, was no longer effective. Manufacturers responded by developing thousands of products for every conceivable market segment.

## What Is Database Marketing?

Database marketing is the art and science of identifying, describing, and locating target segments. Built on the concept of target marketing, database marketing assumes that everyone is *not* your market. Instead, database marketing assumes that smaller, homogeneous segments should be targeted within the massive market structure. For example, the market for cars can be segmented into owners of minivans, domestic cars, foreign cars, red cars, etc. A car dealer who knows how a Lexus owner differs from a Cadillac owner will have a competitive advantage. This is target segmentation.

At the public school level, database marketing assumes that everyone does not love and support public education, although there are smaller, loyal segments. Target segmentation certainly applies here. With database marketing, you can contact one or more groups of your target customer segments for an expressed purpose, which may be to promote a new program's value or gain support for an upcoming budget referendum.

For example, one school system wanted to stimulate participation from the business community for its Lunchtime Read Aloud Program for elementary youngsters. The system obtained a mailing list from the local Chamber of Commerce and sent a mailing to a selective database of businesses—those with more than five employees, those within a reasonable commute to the elementary schools, and those which were involved with the local Chamber of Commerce Business Partnership Program. This targeted approach was more cost effective than mailing to *all* businesses regardless of size, geographic location, or involvement in public education.

## How Does a School System Use Database Marketing?

**Step 1: Generate a current mailing list.** Most public schools have already taken this first step by creating a database. At the very least, schools have student and employee names, addresses, and phone numbers—the beginning of a database and a simple mailing list. Other schools may have mailing information on other customer segments such as parents, grandparents, businesses, and taxpayers.

**Step 2: Enter mailing information on target segments.** The next step is to enter this information (name, address, phone number) into a computerized database software program. A computer consultant will help you determine which of the several software options would best meet your needs.

As soon as you can "call up" the customers' streets, cities, states, zip codes, and phone numbers, you have segmented the marketplace with the help of a computer. Each variable (streets, cities, zip codes, etc.) is called a "field." Each field can be selected out of your database, enabling you to create mailing lists for a specific zip code, state, city, or any other field (or fields) you specify to define the parameters of a list. This is the beauty of the technology. Although this is manually possible, the time required is inordinate and limiting. With the computer, you can practice "target segmentation" with a few keystrokes.

The ability to maintain customer databases on computers is one of the most revolutionary developments in marketing. Human effort could never replicate a computer's efficiency and accuracy. With the software's ability to retrieve or sort customer databases by bits of information on customer segments, your ability to create targeted mailing lists is only limited by the range of customer information in the database. For example, you can communicate with 5th graders who live in a specific neighborhood by telling the computer to find and sort children on grade level (5) with zip code XXXXX. The software program can then generate mailing labels or envelopes.

**Step 3: Add demographic and psychographic profile information.** Database marketing purists would not consider the mailing list data to be "database marketing." Names, addresses, and phone numbers are not enough to truly practice target segmentation to the degree that it becomes a powerful tool. The database must also include strategic descriptive information on each customer. Leadership in this area is needed to determine what additional information you need to meet your marketing goals and objectives.

Schools should set up a planning team to decide what data are needed on each customer segment. What do you already know? What information do you already have in your database? What do you need to know, and how can you obtain these data?

Basic information may cover:
- PTO membership
- Voter registration status
- Political party affiliation
- Voter participation level (active/inactive)
- Number of children in school
- Number of children graduated from school
- Number of preschoolers
- Neighborhood/voting district

More sophisticated databases might have further information on:
- Educational level of parents
- Child's participation in athletics, band, the environmental club
- Newspapers read, employment status, and leisure-time activities

If you had these kind of data in your database, you could select a target segment of parents whose children play basketball, or are in the drama program, from the thousands of children in your system. With a few keystrokes, you can create a complete list or a subsegment list by grade, neighborhood, voter registration, or any other characteristic. This list can be used to generate mailing labels or even personalized letters and envelopes to the target segment of parents for a specific purpose. This is true marketing gold for a school system.

**Step 4: Constantly and meticulously upgrade data.** A database requires constant attention to ensure its accuracy and usefulness. You must input or modify information as it changes. This is especially true with addresses and phone numbers. Database information must be gathered from parents on an annual basis—perhaps every September—with a simple form sent to parents. Add new data and delete old data so the database can be effectively used when needed.

## Why Database Marketing Is the Marketing Gold Mine for Public Schools

Howard Schlossberg of *Marketing News* claims that "behind every great business is an even greater database." A well-developed, maintained database should play an integral role in a school's ability to market itself. It has enormous potential because it offers a highly controllable channel for delivering customized marketing messages to individual target segments.

Whether it is called relationship marketing, frequency marketing, one-to-one marketing, or micromarketing, database marketing enables you to know who your best customers are. This ability is crucial when forming strategic alliances between public schools and target segments of their customers.

The benefits that database marketing brings to public school systems mirror those in the corporate setting.

1. **You can practice powerful target segmentation.** One of the biggest benefits of database marketing is that you can sort, identify, assemble, and communicate with those interested in your school's activities and future plans. Database marketing allows you to go to your supportive customers and offer them a chance for further involvement in or support of your initiatives.

2. **You can develop and maintain long-term relationships with key market segments.** Database marketing helps you maintain and deepen customer loyalty; it can also help you improve relationships with key customers, like the grandparents of students.

3. **You can cross-sell your educational programs.** If a customer segment loves computers, you may be able to cross-sell (or gain support for) this segment on computer clinics, field trips, and other enrichment programs. Because the members of this segment value your computer curricula, you can assume they may also value similar educational programs.

4. **You can extend your product (program) lines.** If a parent group is devoted to computers, you may get its support for a new upgrade in software in future budget requests.

5. **You can approach each customer as an individual, not as a group or collection of customers.** The parent who is sending a first child to kindergarten is very different than the parent who has a teenager in the 11th grade. A targeted approach to the parent segment is much more effective than placing all parents of students in one group.

6. **Your messages will be communicated privately.** If you use the mail (versus the newspaper) to garner support for the middle school referendum from your best customers, your adversaries will not know what you are doing. This is a competitive advantage.

7. **You can reward your best customers.** Database marketing is a way to identify your best customers and reward them for their loyalty. Statistics have shown that 80% of all business is generated by 20% to 25% of your customers.

Is it true that only 20% to 25% of your students' parents attend most of the school events, run most of the PTO activities, buy most of the fund-raising goodies, and most often attend the Board of Education meetings? Wouldn't you like to identify these loyal customers in your database and develop a special relationship with them by rewarding their loyalty?

Give them VIP status when an important event occurs. Appoint them to a commission to determine the need for a new school. Invite them to a luncheon where an author of children's books will speak to your school staff. Have them chair the high school graduation exercises. Send them with your staff to a conference on a "hot topic" in public education. Let them know that their loyalty has been noticed and is appreciated.

## Using Direct Mail Marketing Effectively

How much marketing material did you receive in the mail this week? What percentage went directly into the recycling bin? You may have opened some pieces, but most were probably thrown away in the same shape in which they were sent. Although such junk mail is a minor nuisance for most people, direct mail marketing is a major expense for most businesses and organizations. When it misses its target, direct mail becomes junk mail. You can keep your direct mail pieces on target by following several practical tips.

**Never underestimate the power of an envelope.** Consider the envelopes containing your mail. You don't have to open most of them to know whether you're interested in the contents because the envelopes create an image. This image influences whether or not you will actually open an envelope.

Because this first impression is so important, make sure you use a good tagline (a type of headline) on the outside of the envelope. This tagline will determine 80% of the success of your mailer since it is the invitation to open the envelope and learn more.

A nonstandard envelope, such as a square, may make people curious enough to rip it open. Envelopes that get tossed rather quickly:

- Are #10 business envelopes
- Have a return address the recipient doesn't recognize or care about
- Have a cheshire (preprinted) label
- Are made of cheap, thin paper
- Have the recipient's name misspelled or title incorrect
- Reveal the contents of the letter

Make sure the envelope is visually interesting and compels the recipient to open it: "If it looks like junk, and feels like junk, it must be junk. The extra cost will be well worth the image enhancement value and without a doubt will affect the success of the mailing" (May, 1990).

A preprinted, dot matrix, stick-on label screams out "junk mail inside!" Even though typing or printing every name and address on a laser printer takes time and money, increasing the probability that your target market segment opens the envelope is worth the investment.

**Create a compelling cover letter.** A letter gives you a priceless opportunity to tell your story in warm, human terms. People have been known to read and respond to letters that are 8, 10, or even 15 pages long—but only if they are compelling, according to Rapp and Collins (1987).

The letter should be well written, easy to read, and benefit-oriented. Avoid using arrogant, condescending, or patronizing language and any language that may be considered sexist. Think like the recipient when you review the content of the letter. What will he or she think when reading your letter?

Clearly identify and explain the specific benefits related to your message. If you are asking for volunteers, specify the benefits to the reader. If you are asking for support of a budget referendum, tell the reader why.

**Use a well-sized, uncluttered typeface.** This will be especially appreciated by those with poor eyesight.

**Check and recheck the letter for typos and grammatical errors.** A public school cannot afford these kinds of mistakes.

**Give the reader an opportunity to respond.** According to Rapp and Collins (1987), "running any advertising without offering the public an opportunity to ask for more information seems like a crime." Let the recipient call or write for additional information. This should be easy for school systems and will provide an opportunity to retrieve more information for the target segment database.

**Conduct mailings often.** Don't think that "once in a while" mailings will have any effect. A regular, planned communications program through the mail will help you develop supportive, lasting relationships. The best customers—parents, teachers and other professional staff, the Board of Education—should receive mailings from your school system regularly.

**Customize the message so it is relevant to the recipient.** Consider your audience. Your message to parents will differ from your message to senior citizens. What you say to parents of 3rd graders will differ substantially from what you say to parents of 11th graders.

## Summary

Database marketing involves compiling data on your target market segments in a sophisticated manner and then using the database to provide customized information for marketing efforts. The amount of political clout such marketing can provide is enormous, and the results can be spectacular.

With this tool, you can communicate privately with the friends of public education—parents whose children attend different schools, seniors who have grandchildren in your schools, selected government officials, and other key market segments.

With database marketing, you approach marketing from a relationship standpoint. Properly designed, a sequence of database mailings will add to the database, strengthen old relationships, and develop new ones. The ultimate goal is to bring customers along a loyalty continuum.

Database marketing helps ensure that your customers are well cared for. You are better equipped to retain your current customers and attract new customers. Your circle of supportive customers continually widens. Since getting and keeping customers is the essence of organizational and business health, it is not surprising that some advocates of database marketing claim it can double or even triple your chance for success. It has achieved this for corporations and nonprofit organizations, and it can do it for public education, too.

CHAPTER 7

# USING PROGRAM EVALUATION AS A MARKETING TOOL

In the corporate world, one goal of marketing is to let people know what a company produces. An excellent way to meet this goal in public education is to conduct a program evaluation. Sadly, such evaluation has a negative image within public education since it is often an externally-mandated function and is seen as a punitive effort to uncover program weaknesses.

The negative image also explains why program evaluation is not used by public schools more often as a marketing tool. Instead of being an integral part of programming in the public school system, it is an exception. This is a missed marketing opportunity.

To arrest and reverse the declining image of public education, today's administrators should inform the public about their programs and their efforts to achieve excellence: "If the public's view of education is ever going to change, we must let people know what is going on in our schools and we must keep on letting them know throughout the year" (Blumenthal, 1991).

Peters and Austin (1985) recommend that schools "add enough value to [their] product so that it cannot be resisted. A school is never known by its budget." Showcasing a budget presentation with fancy desktop publishing at public hearings is ludicrous if you stop to think about it. The taxpayer does not want to be faced with a bill. And that is what the budget is—a huge bill, usually about 80% of a town's budget. School systems need to market the benefits of their programs, not showcase the bills for the programs.

Program evaluation is the most effective way to objectively assess the benefits of your programs and provide you with excellent marketing information from answers to questions such as:

1. Which market(s)/customer(s) does this program serve?

2. What are the characteristics of the marketplace?

3. Why is the program being offered? What are the benefits of the program to the market segments/customers?

4. What would make this program better? What can be improved to further satisfy the market segments/customers?

5. What is the level of support for the program? Which target segments/customers support it more and which support it less?

6. Are the benefits of this program worth the expenditure and resources needed to achieve the objectives?

In an urban school system, a dropout prevention program was evaluated for five consecutive years. Each year there were recommendations for program improvement and development. Administrators of the program paid attention to each recommendation, and implemented the changes that were feasible to the fullest extent possible. The program was so strengthened by this evaluation that in the fifth year of pilot funding, the school system could show a significant reduction in the dropout rate for high risk students. Furthermore, the program evaluation demonstrated that students were being promoted (versus retained) to a much higher extent than before program implementation. Systematic program evaluation had shown that the dollar investment in the program had "paid off."

## Summative and Formative Program Evaluations

There are two types of program evaluation: summative and formative (Issac and Michael, 1981).

**Summative evaluation** is *undertaken at the conclusion* of a program—possibly at the end of the pilot year or funding cycle—to document what happened during the program. For example, a high school computer course may be evaluated at the end of the school year to determine its effectiveness in increasing computer literacy in high school students. The information collected may indicate:

1. The number of students served by the course.
2. The required human and technological resources.
3. The degree to which course objectives were obtained.
4. The level of computer literacy gained during the school year.
5. The benefits of the program to students, teachers, parents, and the business community.
6. Improvements that can enhance the program.
7. New programmatic needs.
8. Recommendations for program continuance/discontinuance. (Is there a better alternative?)

**Formative evaluation** produces information *during the development* of the program to assure that the program is progressing as intended. As a monitoring tool, formative evaluation provides in-progress feedback for staff so that adjustments may be made.

For example, formative evaluation seems ideally suited to school systems that include special education students in general education classrooms. The program evaluation might be helpful in:

1. Giving administrators an early indication of the barriers and how they might be removed.
2. Providing information on where the program is working and why, so success can be repeated.
3. Supplying an open communication channel for input during the program.
4. Creating hard data on where the program began and how it developed at critical junctures.
5. Identifying areas of unmet needs or emerging programmatic directions.

## Benefits of Program Evaluation

The benefits are enormous when customer-oriented school systems embrace program evaluation as a key marketing tool.

1. **Program evaluation facilitates program improvement, maximizing the tax dollar investment.** When evaluations are part of a program design, the built-in feedback system will keep staff focused on program goals and objectives. Any problems can be presented through evaluation and then resolved in an expeditious and thoughtful manner.

Over time, program evaluation will stimulate program improvement. The customer receives a better return on the investment/tax dollar and that makes many customers very happy—students, their parents, teachers and staff, taxpayers, and the community.

2. **Program evaluation provides decision-makers with an objective planning and marketing tool for strategic decisions.** Good program evaluation provides excellent decision-making data because it uses research methodology. When program evaluations are conducted, valid, reliable data are systematically obtained, and objective information is generated. The data indicate if the program is working, failing, or in need of repair.

The quality of the information from a good program evaluation is defensible and can withstand the onslaught from external adversarial groups, such as taxpayers associations. School systems need this kind of data muscle throughout the year and especially at budget time when cuts are imminent. Data from a program evaluation report can be very convincing during heated discussions—a powerful weapon that arguments based on emotion or hearsay cannot match.

If administrators come to the Board of Education meetings armed with comprehensive program evaluations of their most vulnerable programs, they can present strong arguments against the random program cuts affecting many education budgets today.

3. **Program evaluation stimulates school systems to move from a product to a customer orientation.** As discussed in Chapter 2, school systems have historically been product oriented. They have believed—with justification—that their product was a good one. Product support was almost assumed.

Today, schools must have a customer orientation to survive and grow. They need to constantly assess how their customers think the programs (products) are doing, rather than congratulate themselves for the great achievements of their programs. Program evaluation data *obtained by asking customers directly* can unequivocally document achievements and prove success to the public school's customers.

Talented and gifted (TAG) programs provide an excellent example of the value of program evaluation. Such programs enjoy a strongly committed support base of students and parents who believe the programs make a difference in the lives of their children. The fact that these programs are routinely being cut from school budgets is partly the fault of those involved in TAG programs for two reasons.

First, the high-quality TAG programs were implemented without a marketing context. The "product" is great, but the marketing to ensure all customers appreciate it is poor or nonexistent. If TAG programs were initially conceived within a marketing context, every concept in this book would have been practiced—from day one. A question to illustrate this point: How many TAG programs practice database marketing? Probably few. The "marketing" actually done for TAG programs has been more promotion, such as newspaper coverage, than an overall marketing strategy as defined in this book. Based on program evaluation, such a marketing strategy begins, continues, and exceeds the life of a program.

Second, program evaluation of TAG programs has been through academic research geared for university audiences, not market research geared for lay audiences. Although academic and market research share the same methods, market research design is based on the customer's point of view, not on that of college faculty members or the peer review board of a particular journal.

In the case of TAG, program evaluation data can be collected from current students, their parents, and alumni of TAG programs. The absence of local TAG evaluations that are research based *and marketing oriented* has led to some of the more tragic losses in this era of budget slashing.

4. **Program evaluation benefits many and helps develop relationships with several customer segments.** Many market segments benefit when school programs are evaluated.

*Program participants and their families—those who directly receive program services.* Students who play soccer, receive flute instruction, learn to paint landscapes, and act in the school musical *Oliver!* are not engaging in so-called "frills." These activities can result in well-rounded students, while bringing a quality of life into their homes, their families, and the community.

***Providers of programs—teachers, support staff, and school personnel.*** Because program evaluation provides an objective, systematic feedback mechanism, there are hard data that can be readily used by staff. Areas for program improvement are identified and strengths are established. Internal renewal occurs, and daily activities are conceived within a framework of goals and objectives.

***Taxpayers—the community at large.*** Those who pay the bill are reassured by the accountability for their money, the built-in monitoring of the program designs, and available information on program strengths and weaknesses. Program evaluation provides a way to measure the return on an investment—something that every taxpayer wants, regardless of age, income, and household composition.

***Elected and appointed local, state, and federal officials.*** Informed decisions can only be made when sound data are provided. Elected officials can support your programs more fully and without hesitation if they have documented proof of program results. Since public officials are subject to tough public scrutiny, they welcome this type of information when faced with issues requiring selection of one among several difficult options.

***Business community—employers.*** The advent of school partnerships has been a mixed blessing for school systems. Although the human and financial resources have been sustaining, the outcomes have often been less than exemplary. This has reinforced the image that educational quality is poor beyond repair and is not worth the tax dollars invested. With program evaluation, the business community will get the hard data it values and use the data to strengthen the partnership, especially if the data concern programs it values—computer education, literacy, basic skills, foreign language, etc.

## Programs That Should Be Evaluated

Given the political climate, the following programs would probably benefit the most from program evaluations:

| | | |
|---|---|---|
| TAG | Foreign language | Special education |
| Drug prevention | Arts | AIDS awareness |
| Music | Violence prevention | Athletics |
| Dropout prevention | Computer | Health |
| ESL | Work study | Advanced Placement |

# Putting Program Evaluation to Work

Program evaluation has many applications and can be used for:

1. **Making a case for program continuance or discontinuance.** School systems need to examine which programs should be discontinued. Not every program needs to or should live forever. Again, program evaluation data will influence such decisions.

*Example:* Ideally, programs designed for dropout prevention, AIDS awareness, and drug prevention will be needed less in the future. Yet, the reality is that violence prevention will likely be needed more in public schools.

2. **Establishing a need for a new program.** Program evaluation data may earmark areas in which new programming should be considered and document outstanding needs in a definitive way.

*Example:* Evaluation of a dropout prevention program may uncover needs that must be met in order to accomplish the overall program goal. Reducing the dropout rate may require pregnancy prevention, childcare provisions, bus money for traveling home after school, or meeting some other need.

3. **Identifying strategy for program revision, adaptation, or change.** The original design of the program may not be the best way to deliver it. Data from a formative program evaluation will provide direction and guidance.

*Example:* Evaluation may indicate that after-school practice time on the computer is the only way 6th graders can achieve total computer literacy. The in-school time is limited, and there are not enough computers for each child to get sufficient amount of instruction. The computer program may achieve better results if it has an after-school adjunct.

4. **Deciding among alternatives.** Unfortunately, all school systems must decide among alternative programs. Program evaluation can provide the data for decision-making by determining the benefits accrued from vulnerable programs and the requisite costs.

*Example:* The lower use rates for the golf program may support arguments for discontinuance in favor of increasing funding for the girls' basketball program. Program evaluations would provide data on use of and funding required for each program.

## Program Evaluation Designs

There are many ways to conduct program evaluations. Those described in Chapter 4 include surveys, focus groups, in-depth interviewing, and field observation. Other designs are described in detail in the numerous textbooks on the market. An excellent reference is the *Handbook of Research and Evaluation* (Issac and Michael, 1981). A few of the more popular evaluation designs are:

**Developmental (longitudinal)**—prospective designs that monitor patterns of growth or change over time. This might be used with an AIDS awareness program to determine the effect on student behavior over a four-year high school career.

**Ex-post-facto (causal comparative)**—retrospective designs that explain relationships by looking to the past. For dropout prevention programs, this design would be an excellent way to explain the causes for dropping out that could be traced to the student's background profile.

**True experimental**—These traditional pre/post designs normally use random selection and assignment of subjects as well as a control group. This is the purest form of research and may be more difficult to implement. This design would be excellent for evaluating a smoking cessation intervention program for staff.

**Quasi-experimental**—This design is similar to a true experimental design but is different in that it relinquishes all control due to extraneous variables. A TAG program might use this design to determine the effect of a special teaching technique on the development of students' writing.

## Summary

Program evaluation is an effective way to gather information on the value of your programs and share information with your customers—students, parents, staff, and the community at large. Sharing such information is one way to counteract the trend listed in Chapter 1 that warned "the public will demand more involvement in public education, yet have little knowledge about how it should be restructured."

If school systems consistently implement evaluation of programs that are vulnerable to cuts, they will be able to provide the steady stream of information needed to ensure that public decision-making is informed and progressive.

CHAPTER 8

# GETTING YOUR MESSAGE TO THE PUBLIC THROUGH MARKETING COMMUNICATIONS

Previous chapters suggest that public education adapt to a changing environment by developing relationships with its key customer segments in the community. Public schools can do so by using marketing communications programs to directly communicate with those segments. Such programs enable schools to create and stimulate interest and concern among the target audience for the public school system.

In the for-profit sector, marketing communications programs are used to promote name recognition and sell more products or services. These programs are effective, because customers are more likely to buy from companies they know about. In public education, familiarity also appears to be correlated with respect and support. According to the 25th Gallup/*Phi Delta Kappan* Poll conducted in 1993, respondents gave A or B ratings to only 19% of the schools across the nation, 47% of the local schools, and an impressive 72% of the schools the respondents were most familiar with—those the respondent's oldest child attended (Elam, 1993). **Support for a school is directly and positively related to how much the public knows about it.**

School administrators are beginning to recognize the importance of informing the public about their school's current and future activities. DeLapp and Smith (1991) contend that "people need to know about our successes, understand our problems and be moved to take action on our behalf." Deede Sharp (1989) stresses the importance of a pervasive and consistent orientation toward talking and listening to the customer:

*Effective schools do not rely on the printed word alone nor do they communicate only through meetings. News is gathered constantly and disseminated through group meetings, as well as one-on-one contacts. News goes to the community through school newspapers, mass media, and a planned public relations program. There is a system, a structured process through which students, teachers and parents know they can express concerns and get response. And the schools listen. They are in tune with their consumers, they have a planned system for gathering data and they are dedicated to keeping their public informed.*

Keeping the community informed is one of the best ways to win community support. It is inexpensive and the benefits are great.

## What Are Marketing Communications?

Marketing communications are tools used for persuasive communication. Their major purpose in public schools is to provide information to and develop relationships with customers.

An excellent example of marketing communications was produced by the staff of the San Bernardino County Superintendent of Schools office. It condensed the cumbersome 176-page annotated report entitled *Perspectives on Education in America* into a set of 22 overhead transparencies and handouts entitled "Public Education: Making Its Mark." By focusing on five topics important to the customers of public education, this marketing communications piece left an indelible message.

Marketing communications programs can benefit a public school system in many ways by:

- Creating a deeper awareness
- Generating interest
- Informing and educating
- Establishing credibility
- Boosting reputation and image
- Giving wide visibility
- Promoting important programs and services
- Developing a communication link with the community
- Enhancing relationships

Of the many components of the complex marketing communications field, three general types of marketing communications seem well-suited to school systems: advertising, publicity, and personal contact.

# ADVERTISING

A simple definition of advertising is *purchased time or space to communicate promotional information.* You control the message because you pay for it. Advertising may be funded by the public school, the Board of Education, a PTO, the town or city, a PAC, the realtors' group, the Chamber of Commerce, a local corporation or business, the Rotary Club, or a nonprofit agency.

## Traditional Advertising

Public school proponents might use traditional advertising in newspapers or on TV and radio if there is an upcoming vote on a facilities expansion or when the community needs information on something important to the school system. Public schools that use the following six-step process will increase the effectiveness of their advertising.

1. **Plan the specific objectives of the advertising campaign.** Exactly what are you trying to achieve? These objectives should be written down and they should be measurable. Remember, you will spend precious dollars with any advertising effort—be accountable. Objectives should be framed around two essential questions:

- What is the desired outcome?
- Who is the target customer for the message?

2. **Determine your advertising budget.** How much can you afford to spend? Do you need corporate underwriters? Make sure your budgeted amount is established and recorded.

(A note on the politics of advertising and image: Consider all advertising expenditures for their marketing benefits *and* potential effect on image. For example, a TV commercial is perceived as expensive advertising, and your school system may be seen as wasting tax money.)

3. **Develop the theme and message to be communicated.** Each advertising initiative should be built around a central, unifying theme or

idea. The theme should focus on the objective and should be interesting, desirable, distinctive, and believable.

After developing the theme, develop the message to support it. The message should focus on the recipient (the target audience), not the sender (the public school). In advertising, the message is called "copy."

Avoid developing only one message if you need to reach multiple market segments. Your appeal to households with school-aged children must be different than your appeal to senior citizens. The message will differ, but the theme should be the same: "Tailor your message and your approach to best meet their needs. A communications program won't work very well when it practices 'Ready, fire, aim'" (DeLapp and Smith, 1991).

4. **Focus on headline development.** Headlines are very, very important. Readers will often scan them to determine if they will read the message. The headline is the invitation to read the message—make it as compelling as possible by keeping the following in mind:

- **A longer, more informative headline is better than a short, cute, and awkward one.** Be specific. Don't be funny. You are not trying to entertain; you are informing, educating.

- **Don't ask a question.** No one should have to think of the answer—don't make the reader work.

- **Use a simple typeface and a large enough type size for the readers.** If the elderly are part of the market, remember that vision fails with age. Small type sizes and script and italics typefaces are harder to read and should be avoided.

- **If you use a picture or visual, it should convey the same message as the headline.** The four advertisements on the following pages were used for passage of a middle school referendum. The theme was "We need a new middle school." The submessages were (1) the enrollment crisis will worsen over the next five years, (2) the new school will cost less than renovating the old school, (3) alternative proposals are inadequate and are not cheaper, and (4) we need to do something now.

Each advertisement has a powerful, declarative headline. The messages are informative, simple, easy to read, and repeated throughout. Visuals are

*Getting Your Message to the Public through Marketing Communications*

clear and reinforce the message. The school also considered its image and budget needs by securing funding for each advertisement from one of the local corporations.

## FACT #1 FOR A NEW MIDDLE SCHOOL:

# A NEW Middle School will COST LESS Than Renovating Vogel-Wetmore.

Compare the costs in these two tables:

|  | **NEW Middle School** | Renovating Vogel-Wetmore |
|---|---|---|
| Cost | **$25 Million** | $20 Million |
| State Reimburses | **72%** | 50%* |
| Taxpayer's Actual Cost | **$7 Million** | $10 Million |

*According to State Department of Education

| Taxes Required[1] | |
|---|---|
| **NEW Middle School** | **$34 per year** |
| Renovate Vogel-Wetmore | $49 per year |

[1] On $100K of assessed property value; average payment based on 20-year bond, including interest

**VOTE FOR A NEW MIDDLE SCHOOL!**

FACT #2 FOR A NEW MIDDLE SCHOOL:

# Alternative "Solutions" are Not Adequate and Do Not Cost Less.

**DOUBLE SESSIONS**
at Vogel-WetMore will cost approximately
$1.3 MILLION MORE each year with
NO STATE REIMBURSEMENT.

**PORTABLE CLASSROOMS**
will each cost $56,575 EACH YEAR to rent
and WILL NOT ADD more lunch room,
library or gym space. In addition, there
would be NO STATE REIMBURSEMENT.

## VOTE FOR A NEW MIDDLE SCHOOL!

*Getting Your Message to the Public through Marketing Communications*

---

**FACT #3 FOR A NEW MIDDLE SCHOOL:**

# We Already Have an Enrollment Crisis at Vogel-Wetmore.

**Actual Enrollment Growth at Vogel-Wetmore**

This graph shows only students already in the Torrington School System. It does not account for additional students projected beyond these numbers.

| '90-'91 | '91-'92 | '92-'93 | '93-'94 | '94-'95 | '95-'96 | '96-'97 |
|---|---|---|---|---|---|---|
| 935 | 989 | 1057 | 1070 | 1113 | 1150 | 1215 |

--- 772 STUDENTS VOGEL-WETMORE CAPACITY ---

## VOTE FOR A NEW MIDDLE SCHOOL!

# You Have an Important Decision to Make Today.

**PLEASE CONSIDER THESE FACTS CONCERNING A NEW MIDDLE SCHOOL:**

FACT 1. Today there are hundreds more students at Vogel-Wetmore than it was recommended to handle; it will get even more overcrowded every year.

FACT 2. The State is committed to providing 72%, or $18 million towards construction of a new school.

FACT 3. The cost to taxpayers of renovating Vogel-Wetmore would be $10 million, while building a modern new middle school would cost only $7 million after state reimbursements.

FACT 4. The alternatives to the construction of a new school could cost taxpayers millions of dollars each year and we will not receive any reimbursement from the state.

## Come On, Torrington! WE CAN DO IT!

*Getting Your Message to the Public through Marketing Communications*

On the other hand, the opposition's ads were confusing, complex, and visually unappealing.

---

**VOTERS OF THE CITY OF TORRINGTON
IT'S TIME TO CONTROL MUNICIPAL SPENDING**

# VOTE NO

**ON THE PROPOSED NEW MIDDLE SCHOOL
AND SWIMMING POOL**
MONDAY, DECEMBER 17, 1990
6:00 a.m. to 8:00 p.m.
**CITY HALL AUDITORIUM**

STARTING JANUARY 1ST AND CONTINUING FOR THE NEXT UNKNOWN NUMBER OF YEARS YOUR TAXES ARE GOING TO INCREASE TO COVER THE COSTS OF THE FOLLOWING ITEMS, THE TOTAL OF WHICH CAN REACH CLOSE TO $90 MILLION DOLLARS.

1. CONSIDER: CITY LONG TERM INDEBTEDNESS AS OF 12-10-90 IS $30,000,000 INTEREST NOT INCLUDED.
   ON GOING EXPANSION OF SEWER SYSTEM???
   RECYCLE PROGRAM???
2. SEWAGE TREATMENT PLANT IN THE RANGE OF $30,000,000*
3. CLEAN UP NAUGATUCK RIVER IN THE RANGE OF $10-$15 MILLION.*
4. RUWET'S 26 ACRES TO BE "SOLD" TO THE CITY OF TORRINGTON AT A COST OF $76,923 PER ACRE.
   OF THE 61 ACRES "DONATED", 22 ACRES ARE CLASSIFIED AS WETLANDS. DO WE KNOW WHAT THE LAND VALUE IS AT TODAY'S MARKET???
5. ARCHITECTS FEES .................................................. $1,320,000 OR 6 PERCENT.
   CONSTRUCTION MANAGER FEES ............................ $ 746,000 or 4 PERCENT.
6. PROPOSED SWIMMING POOL...COST $1,800,000 DOES NOT INCLUDE INTEREST OVER THE PERIOD OF THE BONDS.
   50 PERCENT STATE REIMBURSEMENT.
   MAINTENANCE COST OF THE NEW POOL $150,000 PER YEAR.
   RENTING THE YMCA POOL COST BETWEEN $50-$55,000 PER YEAR.
7. PROPOSED MIDDLE SCHOOL... TOTAL COST INCLUDING PRINCIPAL AND INTEREST, OVER THE PERIOD OF THE BONDS, IN THE RANGE OF $48,000,000.*
   WITH A 72.14 PERCENT REIMBURSEMENT THE CITY'S SHARE WILL BE $13,000,000.
8. BONDING FOR THE NEW SCHOOL HAS NOT BEEN VOTED UPON BY THE FINANCE REVENUE BONDING COMMITTEE IN HARTFORD AS OF 12-10-90. FOR VERIFICATION CALL MR. DAVID WEDGE STATE DEPARTMENT OF EDUCATION. 1-566-7548
   WHAT IMPACT WILL BE PLACED ON TORRINGTON TAXPAYERS IF THE STATE DEFAULTS???

*interest cost included.*

PAID FOR BY THE TORRINGTON TAXPAYERS ASSOCIATION

**5. Determine which advertising media will best meet your needs.** Common advertising media include newspaper, TV, radio, magazines, and outdoor advertising. You may want to use 60% newspaper advertisements and 40% local cable TV commercials. Circulation/readership rates and audience characteristics are important considerations. If you are targeting the elderly and you use TV advertisements, you might not reach 75% of the audience, most of whom religiously read the local newspaper.

You must also decide which *media vehicles* to use. If you choose newspapers, should you advertise in the local or county-wide newspaper? Base these decisions on what your target market reads most frequently.

Finally, you must determine the *timing* of your ads. Would running ads once a month, in a one-week period, or spaced throughout just one edition of a newspaper be the best strategy? Try to get professional advice when making this decision.

**5. Evaluate the effect of the advertising on the target market** by pretesting and post-testing your advertising.

*Pretest your advertising.* A leader in advertising, David Ogilvy (1985), warns that "you don't stand a tinker's chance of producing successful advertising unless you start by doing your homework." Pretesting is critical before launching your advertising campaigns. Do not be afraid to show your ad to an objective sample of the target market before you run it. Is the message clear, easy to read, factual, visually appealing, and not offensive? Their feedback will help you improve the ad. Those who ignore such research "are as dangerous as generals who ignore decodes of enemy signals" (Ogilvy, 1985).

*Post-test your advertising.* Determine the ad's effect after it is released. Focus on the only really important question: *Did the ad accomplish its objective?* Did it inform, educate, change attitudes, gain support? Evaluation can be as informal as asking at a meeting, "What do you think of XYZ?"

The post-test response is very important and can help you refine or change the message to make it more effective. View such evaluation as an opportunity for improving the next step in your campaign. If a certain tool does not have the desired effect, changing the tool may dramatically improve your chance of success.

## Outreach Materials

Many school systems have heavily used this type of advertising for years. Although they have called these marketing pieces "outreach materials," any printed or audio-visual materials prepared to influence the public's image of the school system and develop awareness and interest may be considered advertising.

Outreach materials can include information sheets, brochures, business cards, stationery, pamphlets, annual reports, posters, directories, catalogs, videotapes, or newsletters. When you consider how many outreach pieces your school system uses, and how each affects your image, reviewing the quality of each piece should become an important part of your strategic marketing effort.

**A few examples.** A simple *fact sheet* explaining five reasons why a child deserves "another year" before starting kindergarten can be an inexpensive and highly effective way to communicate with parents of preschoolers.

A district-wide *brochure* can discuss the schools in the system—statistics, programs, achievements, key individuals, special events, etc.—and can be given to businesses, realtors, new parents, new families, and others to increase familiarity with the school district.

A bimonthly *newsletter* covering your school's accomplishments and activities can strengthen community relationships. To keep costs down, distribution can be limited to the families who have children in your schools.

Volunteers with technical expertise can produce a *videotape* highlighting a school program or addressing a topic of concern. (Don't forget to first determine these topics through market research.) A few examples might be:

- How to apply to college and get financial aid
- How to write a good term paper
- How to get parents more involved in school
- How to get your child to read and write more often

All outreach pieces must have established goals and objectives. Far too often, exciting logos and fancy slogans are developed around a conference table by well-intentioned people wanting to do something. Although producing outreach materials makes everyone feel good because the materials seem to help, the time and money required for these efforts should be devoted to achieving a marketing goal which focuses on the receiver's, not the sender's, viewpoint.

**Avoid logo-itis.** Ignorance about marketing has created fervent adulation for the symbols of marketing, especially the logo. These graphic symbols usually include a slogan or a Latin phrase which few understand. If the logo doesn't convey the unique identity and mission of your school system to the customer, it has failed.

A second problem occurs when one school system uses several logos. This can only confuse your customers—choose the most effective logo and use it repeatedly. Consistency of image will make the logo memorable and meaningful.

If you have a logo, or are thinking about using one, field-test it by asking a representative sample of your customers the following questions: What does this logo mean to you? What image is conveyed?

## Merchandising

Your school can also promote name recognition and customer loyalty through merchandising—giving away or selling refrigerator magnets, calendars, T-shirts, clothing, cups, or other items bearing your school's name and logo. A sports team that sells hats and shirts with its name and logo is using merchandising. The primary purpose of merchandising is to develop customer loyalty by keeping your name in front of the target audience.

## PUBLICITY

Publicity involves gathering, developing, and spreading the good news about your school system to your customers. The news can be *anything of possible interest* and/or *something that the public does not know and might want to*. According to Williams (1993), "much of what people know about their local schools doesn't come from the teachers, the principal or even the superintendent. It comes from news reports."

Unlike paid advertising, publicity includes obtaining free editorial space in media which are read, viewed, or heard (newspapers and magazines, TV and radio, etc.).

## Newspapers

Newspapers can provide publicity for the public school by printing press releases they receive from the school or by printing articles reporters have written about your school. Publicity may be obtained on numerous topics, including:

- Appointment of new personnel
- Student or staff awards
- New programs
- Grant funding, staff publications
- Test scores and college placement
- Student employment
- School-based studies or surveys
- Special events
- Community involvement

## TV and Radio

Your community cable access network and local radio stations can also provide free publicity. Develop relationships with the key individuals responsible for these media, and you might be able to have school events broadcast, feature a staff member with special skills, provide a panel discussion on teaching sex education in school, or have a call-in show in which you are available to answer questions from the community. Sawyer and Matsumoto (1993) describe other excellent publicity opportunities.

## Getting Publicity Is Not Easy

Many public schools have to rely on publicity because of limited funds for other advertising options. But getting publicity does require effort. You must be successful in *obtaining* news coverage. Because publicity is free, the media control coverage frequency, extent, and focus. This means that a negative story may emerge even if the outlet uses your positive press release.

## Publicity Requires Homework

To increase the likelihood of positive, frequent publicity, the public school system should follow a three-step process:

1. **Define the objectives of the publicity event by identifying what marketing objective you want to accomplish.**

2. **Brainstorm all of the ways a story can be told to accomplish your marketing objective.** If your music program faces cutbacks, your marketing objective may be simply "to document the benefits of the music program." The next step is to have the staff brainstorm ideas on how this "story" could be told.

3. **Develop a strong relationship with newspaper, TV, and radio reporters** so that you have someone to issue stories to and someone who will cover your news. How will reporters know about a children's author visiting your elementary school? Tell them by sending what is known as a "tip sheet" to announce an upcoming special event. Use follow-up phone calls to see if reporters are interested or need more information.

You probably have hundreds of interesting stories you could provide the media. Are there any especially gifted students or faculty members in your school system? Upcoming special events? Recent awards or achievements? As you choose among them, remember that each story should have a marketing objective and should be conceived and developed within a marketing context. Ask whether a story will positively promote your school. If the answer is "yes," tell it!

## PERSONAL CONTACT

### Public Speaking

**Make it everyone's responsibility.** Public speaking is an excellent and inexpensive, but underused, way to get the message out. You should take every opportunity possible to speak about your schools and their accomplishments.

The job descriptions of superintendents, principals, teachers, and staff should include the responsibility to tell the community what they are doing and how these activities will benefit the community. This will help the customers understand and appreciate the many returns on their tax dollar investment.

School administrators and staff can convey your message to the public through a speakers' bureau or attendance at various community gatherings. Gatherings can be as diverse as Chamber of Commerce meetings and daycare centers—any gathering that includes members of your target audience. Not only does public speaking foster goodwill within the community, it also provides the school system with significant control over the message—a major benefit. Another strategy is to meet regularly with active community leaders to establish and build public support.

**Orientation is critical.** Be sure to provide an orientation for your speakers. These image emissaries need to understand their role in this venture.

First, speakers must be reminded that all citizens are customers and must be treated in a kind and sensitive manner no matter what they say about the public school. You never win an argument with the customer and should never try to. This lesson must especially be emphasized when the speaker's message has a political overtone.

Second, the nature of the speech should be clarified before it is ever given. Are speakers presenting a case for a new school or delivering a talk on how to use a word processor to help a child do term papers? These two topics require different orientations by administrators. Remember, the goals and objectives of public speaking efforts should be preplanned and thoughtfully executed. Share your expectations with your public speakers and provide guidance on what they should and should not do or say.

Finally, you should also address how the school's image can be affected by the appearance and behavior of the speaker and by the appearance of any handouts or materials used in the presentation. A speaker whose shirt is not tucked in or one who says "um" repeatedly will give the audience a negative image of your school. Worse, that speaker may be the only contact these customers have with you, and that experience will likely be repeated to others. Your speakers must understand that the school's image is affected by the messenger and the medium as well as the message.

## Special Events Management

When schools consider promoting themselves, most think of advertising with brochures and direct-mail pieces. Although special events management rarely comes to mind, schools can easily use a planned occasion for a targeted customer segment to stimulate media interest and garner publicity.

Special events, such as an ice cream social, occur in school systems *all year round,* and many are outstanding marketing opportunities. These opportunities are often lost because the parents, staff, and students get so much joy from the special event that they don't see it as a way to build support for their school district, school, or program.

**The ice cream social.** During an elementary school's annual ice cream social, parents and children pack the school gym, playing games that teachers and PTO members devised. The children love the prizes, and people are walking around, happily chatting with one another. After the games, everyone gets an ice cream sundae. It is a spectacularly successful event. The school is perceived as a place where the whole family wants to be.

This "feel-good" special event could have been scripted in a book on public relations. Several aspects of the event could have been integrated into the elementary school's marketing efforts:

1. **An "I Love My Grandparent" raffle could be held.** Each child receives a free chance to win by filling out cards with their grandparents' names and addresses. After the event, the school uses the cards to develop a mailing database for future use in developing a relationship with this market segment and encouraging support of fund-raising, program development, budget referenda, and other school activities.

2. **The table holding the ice cream could also display literature on school programs vulnerable to cuts** (with names and numbers of school personnel who could provide more information). A district brochure and the school newsletter could also be placed on this table.

3. **A table could be discreetly placed in the gym for voter registration.** Many parents are not registered to vote—you need their support.

4. **A VIP booth could be set up so parents can discuss their concerns with school administrators, teachers, and other staff.**

Special events should be designed with clear-cut marketing goals in mind. If your goal is to raise money for an upcoming referendum political action committee (PAC), you might host a special fund-raising event instead of asking for donations. Special events *provide a marketing exchange* that provides customers with an immediate benefit.

**A few more examples.** A school could host a visit from a famous childrens' book author. For a reasonable fee, anyone can have breakfast with and meet the author. In this exchange, the school raises money and gets good publicity, attendees get to meet and hear a famous author, and the author gets paid to promote and sell books.

A school that holds a spaghetti or pot luck supper for parents at the beginning of the school year has a captive audience for any message it wants to deliver. This time should be used by the Board of Education and the school system to identify themselves, address the goals and challenges of the upcoming school year, and answer questions of parents in attendance. If parents eat, meet the staff, and go home, you have lost a valuable marketing opportunity.

Every school event should be considered with an eye toward marketing the school or school system. Messages should be delivered, relationships should be developed, and the press should always be invited to attend.

## Summary

With a formal marketing communications plan, a school can develop its image in a methodical, proven way. Advertising, publicity, and personal contact can be used to effectively tell a positive story about your school.

Never underestimate the value of a marketing communications program. It can do far more than simply describe a school district, school, or program. It creates and reinforces your image, develops an awareness of who you are, and promotes school goals and objectives. It influences elected officials and generates support from target audiences, especially from those who oppose public school goals.

Cannon and Barnham (1993) suggest that "perceptions of public education are rooted in people's personal experience and direct understanding of their local schools." This is a simple, powerful fact. Executed correctly, the marketing communications program can increase community interaction with and knowledge of your school system and ensure the community support your school system needs.

**CHAPTER 9**

# MARKETING COMMUNICATION STRATEGIES

Whether you use advertising, publicity, or personal contact to get your message to the public, using the following eight strategies will increase the effectiveness and quality of your marketing communications program.

## Strategy #1: Seize All Opportunities that Communicate Quality to the Customer

Customers feel good when they believe they are getting a quality product for a reasonable cost. The need to emphasize quality has become acute as public education has become more and more expensive. Schools must begin to use marketing communications to highlight quality. This can be difficult.

Quality means different things to different customer segments. Think about what quality means to someone who owns a Mercedes Benz versus a Corvette, a Ford truck versus a Honda Civic. Each market segment has a different definition of quality.

The same is true for public education. Quality is not a homogeneous concept to elementary, middle, and secondary school students; their parents and grandparents; the teachers and staff; the elderly; business leaders and government officials; and other customers.

Does quality mean perfect attendance, academic honors, no budget increases, high college placement, no graffiti on the walls, job placement rates, literacy, no drug use, after-school job performance, clean school grounds, or energy conservation? Public schools need to determine what quality means to each key market segment and then use the marketing communications tools in the Appendix to make the school's quality come alive to its target segments of customers.

In order to have any meaning, quality should be defined in ways customers understand and value. If quality means high academic achievement to several customer segments, you may want to "showcase" those students who make the honor roll and receive awards and distinctions. Ceremonies, announcements, and the more traditional ways of celebrating these accomplishments need to be expanded. Notify parents with a handwritten note from the principal. Give the students a pizza party, an extra free period, a ribbon or pin. Place their pictures in the hallways for all visitors to see. Display a banner outside the school that lists the names of students who make high honors.

All of these small efforts count and pay huge dividends in improving school image.

## Strategy #2: Identify All Customer Segments that Should Hear the Good News about Your School System

An excellent article by Robinson (1991) underscores a theme of this book. When you consider who to inform about your school, you need to consider target segments in your customer population, especially key opinion leaders/influents, parents, the nonparent community, and employees.

**Key opinion leaders/influents.** Depending on the size of the community, Robinson suggests that smart school systems generate a list of 50, 100, or even 500 community and parent opinion-makers. These individuals should be sent board meeting highlights, briefings on the district's budget and other issues before the board, negotiation highlights, the district's annual report, and the district newsletter. She also advises the strategy of sending this group special mailings if rumor control is needed.

This list should be kept up-to-date at all times. Volunteers on various community boards do change. Make sure you have the current name with the current affiliation on your computerized database list and at your fingertips with a current printout. Howlett (1993) underscores the value of this strategy by urging schools to "keep these school district advocates informed, alert and 'on call.' Use them as your community sounding board, information resource and reality check."

**The parent community.** Robinson suggests visiting the parents' homes and distributing newsletters from principals. Make time for important personal contact. Host a first-Friday-of-the-month morning "coffee and donuts" before work for parents or an after-school ice cream social once a month for children and the parents who are picking them up. Spend time chatting to groups while they indulge in a donut or sundae.

**The nonparent community.** Superintendent Robinson sends a welcome letter to all new businesses in her target geographic market area, also enclosing school district news and annual reports. She invites the business community to a luncheon that focuses on what it needs from educated employees, not on what schools need from businesses. She has established a liaison with religious and community groups and has a continuous outreach program to these diverse market segments to bring them into the school system's circle of friends.

**Employees.** Employees are your key public school ambassadors to the community. Information that affects the employees and their school systems should be disseminated to them regularly and fully. The staff should never be the last ones to know about something that affects them directly or indirectly. Keep them informed, and they will serve you and the community well.

Don't fall victim to believing "they don't need to know." You work in a public setting governed by state and federal laws, including the Freedom of Information Act. Err on the side of open communications, judiciously delivered, and you will strengthen ties to your best allies.

## Strategy #3: Use Repetition to Make Your Message Memorable

The value of repetition can best be understood when you realize that "you aren't advertising to a standing army; you are advertising to a moving parade" (Ogilvy, 1985). Delivering your message once is not enough to make it memorable and feasible. You must repeat it.

An excellent example appeared in the *Wall Street Journal,* which was attempting to show the value of repeat advertising. In their ad, there were nine pictures of an Irish setter. Under eight of the nine pictures, the caption said, "Sit," but the dog continued to stand. Under the ninth picture, the caption said, "Good dog." Finally, after hearing the command eight times, the dog sat.

## Strategy #4: Develop a Solid Relationship with the Media

Robinson (1991) urges educators to "work diligently to be accessible to the media" and "give them clear, consistent and accurate information, honor their deadlines, and prepare background information on complex issues."

**Do your homework well.** Find out what radio and TV stations, newspapers, and community magazines cover your school *and* what their target audiences are. Compile a list of the names, addresses, and phone numbers of media and the specific reporters and photographers that cover your area.

Review the sections in which different media publish stories on public education and read the last six months of these sections to determine what was covered, by whom, and how. Also, note the photographers who cover educational stories. Get information on deadlines, editorial schedules, policies on news coverage, public service announcements, and any other media requirements.

Ensure your information is always accurate and newsworthy. Busy newspaper editors cannot afford to waste time on ho-hum stories or desperate attempts to get coverage. Most of all, be honest, reliable, and straightforward. Answer questions fully and candidly or refer to the person who can fill in the gaps. Always remember to thank the media representatives; they are doing you a favor by covering your school or school system.

**Practice good media relations.** Siegle (1989) and Williams (1993) give the following wise advice for developing an effective relationship with the media:

1. Return calls from reporters as soon as you can and give your home phone number so that you can be reached after business hours.

2. Don't bluff the answer; find out and call back. Always be truthful.

3. Don't go off the record with a reporter unless you know and trust him or her.

4. Don't tell a reporter how to write the story.

5. Avoid educational jargon or acronyms that only select audiences can understand.

6. Give documentation or information packets to supplement what the reporter is covering.

7. Never cover up. It will be seen as dishonest and will permanently affect future credibility.

8. Correct any inaccuracies in a story, but do not object to the tone. That is the writer's prerogative.

9. Don't assume you can review articles. If needed, check facts over the phone. Reporters do not have the time to have a reviewer outside of their own offices.

10. Give compliments when they are due by writing to a reporter's supervisor.

11. Be aware that any report or survey developed with public tax dollars is public information.

A little "schmoozing" doesn't hurt either. Mulkey (1993) suggests you "invite reporters to a continental breakfast and then give them updates on district expenditures, programs, and upcoming events."

## Strategy #5: Name an EdMarketing Coordinator

Delapp and Smith (1991) stress that "the best public relations are personal relations. It's easy to be unfair to an entity or a faceless school bureaucrat. It's a lot harder to be unfair to someone you know." If the content in this book is to be fully implemented, school systems may need to designate an EdMarketing Coordinator. If possible, this should be a full-time or part-time professional position, separate from other positions in the school system. Where the feasibility is limited, the Coordinator may be a current full-time or part-time staff member who might receive supplemental compensation.

In large school systems *each school* in the system may need to have a separate, designated *liaison* who reports to the Coordinator at the central district office. In smaller school systems, the Coordinator may be able to cover adequately each school in the system.

The Coordinator should meet with newspaper editors to learn the rules of getting into print, including deadlines, formats, size, color and quality of photos, and substance. He or she should stay in touch with editors and invite them to the school for special events. The Coordinator should also give the editor phone numbers and times during the day when he or she is available so that accessibility is not a problem. Giving the home phone number may be a good idea to consider.

Creating this position benefits the school in other ways besides increasing coverage in the newspaper. Giving one person the responsibility for coordinating communication means that information dissemination is consistent, clean, and thoughtful.

To use this person effectively, the school superintendent has to establish with staff the fact that all information to the press (and queries from the press) must go through this person. Those who answer the phone should understand that the Coordinator must get messages *immediately*, not at the end of the school day when misinformation or rumors have had a chance to spread.

All phone calls from the newspaper should be returned *immediately*. This will help the editor become comfortable with one individual and will clearly express the expectation that he/she is the first person contacted by the media. Misunderstandings will be avoided and a productive relationship between the school and the press will be forged. The editor will also know who to call if a school issue emerges or a teacher in the system becomes newsworthy.

Although the Coordinator has specific and unique responsibilities, marketing is everyone's job. Everyone is an image emissary and should be trained and rewarded based on their ability and willingness to implement a customer-oriented marketing philosophy.

*Marketing Communication Strategies*

# Strategy #6: Issue Press Releases and PSAs

**Press releases.** The Coordinator should write and issue regular press releases. A good press release answers the journalistic questions of:

- Who?
- What?
- Where?
- When?
- How?
- Why?

Press releases are usually one to two pages, typed on standard-size paper. A sample press release is provided on page 114. The first page of a press release should be on school letterhead or on a page that clearly identifies the source of the press release. At the very top of the first page in the upper left or righthand corner, type:

FOR IMMEDIATE RELEASE *or* FOR RELEASE (*date*)

The most important information should be in the first paragraph since your press release will be edited for size and content from the bottom up. Short sentences will be appreciated. Leave some space at the top of the first page for the editor to make notes and develop a headline. (You should always include a title, though.)

Give a clean, well-presented, thoroughly researched, correctly spelled version of the press release to the editor. Remember, press releases are free publicity. Save the editor time and the school potential embarrassment by ensuring press releases are as error-free as possible. Provide a photo or two. Double-space the text. Have someone proofread the release. Include the name and phone of the contact person (the Coordinator) for any follow-up.

Write the press release before the event—old news is no news. You could also make a follow-up phone call after you send the release to answer any questions.

**PSAs.** Radio and TV offer air time for public service announcements (PSAs). These provide a useful way of giving short, factual information about school events or policies.

**NEWS RELEASE**
Westin Public Schools
126 Migeon Ave.
P.O. Box 1444
Westin, NY 10889

**FOR IMMEDIATE RELEASE**
September 15, 1994
*For more information contact:*
Joanne Calafiore
(212) 344-8977

## PEER MEDIATION REDUCES VIOLENCE IN CITY SCHOOLS

Superintendent Dr. Anne Lennon announced today that the Peer Mediation Program conducted over the past three years in the Westin Public Schools has had a significant impact on reducing the violence in the city's schools. The findings of the recent evaluation by Words and Numbers Research, Inc., documented a measurable effect in reducing the incidence of fighting and the number of fighting-related suspensions.

The Peer Mediation Program provides 15 hours of training to students in the basics of conflict resolution and then assigns students to mediate conflicts among their peers. Peer mediations typically deal with interracial incidents, property thefts, and disputes involving gossip, name calling, and threats. The program began in 1990 with a private foundation grant and will conclude in 1995. Since its inception, 425 middle and high school students have been trained as peer mediators. They have participated in 568 cases, of which 494 (or 87%) were successful with written agreements between disputing students.

"I am convinced that the Peer Mediation Program provides our students with an alternative way of resolving their problems rather than verbal or physical conflicts," said Dr. Lennon. "Our students now feel that they have some control over their problems and are buying into the program." Dr. Lennon reported that the positive outcomes have reinforced the Board of Education's long-range goal of increasing the number of peer mediators by 25% over the next two years.

PSAs should take no longer than 10, 30, or 60 seconds to read. After writing a PSA, ask one of your colleagues to review it. Is it easy to say the words you chose? Does it flow? Does it make sense to a non-educator? When issuing PSAs, give the dates they should be aired and then discontinued.

## Strategy #7: Start Building an Arsenal in Writing and in Pictures

**Letters to the editor.** Don't underestimate the power of a good letter to change attitudes and improve the school system's image. Your staff, Board of Education members, students, and parents can contribute to your marketing communications effort by writing letters to the editor, which are often published and widely disseminated.

Reprinted on the following pages are three actual letters to the editor on a new middle school referendum in a community with a disproportionately large elderly voter segment. Letters A and B are developed with the voter in mind. Their messages are short and clear and have been positioned to appeal to the voter who does not want to spend extra tax dollars on a new school.

Unfortunately, there are far more letters like Letter C on the Editorial Page today, demonstrating the opposition's ability to mobilize its forces and write, write, write.

# Letter A

To the Editor:

Now that the election is finally over, those of us who believe in quality education should focus all of our efforts on next month's referendum on the new middle school.

No one can argue that we do not have need for a new middle school. Opponents who argue that we do not have a need for this school have distorted the facts.

So the only rational argument left for the opponents of the new middle school is cost.

The cost for the new school has been reduced significantly. Everything that is now included in the estimated cost for the new middle school is absolutely necessary, in order to provide a quality education for our children.

The state will be paying for 72 percent of the cost, in the event that it should be approved in the December referendum.

The state is broke. We should take advantage of this 72 percent contribution while we still have this available to us.

Everyone who believes that we must provide quality education for our children should work very hard to convince their friends, relatives, neighbors, and co-workers to vote in favor of the new school, so we will continue to provide our children with an equal opportunity to succeed in life.

R. Anthony Wall, Jr.

*Register Citizen* 1990

# Letter B

To the Editor:

I am a stingy taxpayer who supports the new middle school. This is why. A new school will cost me less, not more, in taxes than renovating. Specifically, costs are 9 cents a day for a new school versus 13 cents a day for an old, renovated school. For me, this is a simple, economic decision.

Whether we like it or not, the town must educate its burgeoning school-age population who cannot fit in existing facilities. The same premise applied when the need for the Senior Center emerged. Whether the town liked it or not, we have a burgeoning 65+ population to serve and did so willingly with tax dollars.

Now the Taxpayers Association (a misnomer if there ever was one) is teaching our children a pitiful lesson. Members are telling us to pay $1 for a day-old donut when we can buy a freshly-made one for 50 cents. What kind of foolish advice is that?

Put the extra dollars back in your pocket while the State is being so generous with a 72 percent reimbursement rate. (This exceptional offer is time limited.) That is why I am voting "Yes" on December 17th. The new middle school is the cheaper and better choice—no ifs, ands, or buts.

Susan Rovezzi-Carroll

*Register Citizen* 1990

## Letter C

> To the Editor:
>
> The Board of Education is like a runaway train. Its actions through the years, from closing four neighborhood and well-built schools and hiring numerous teachers' aides to granting exorbitant pay raises, are not enough. Now the board has granted a staggering salary to the new school superintendent.
>
> The manner in which pay raises and salaries are granted begs for changing. City boards can grant pay raises and salaries without needing to give taxpayers advance notice of the figure. The setup is antithetical to democracy; discussion and debate are stifled.
>
> The Charter Revision Commission might care to propose that a public hearing be held prior to the adoption of pay raises and salaries. Either that or the Taxpayers Association might want to conduct a petition of recall. One way or the other, we must stop this train before it takes us over the cliff.
>
> Thomas Bado
>
> *Register Citizen* 1990

**Columns, articles, Op-Ed pieces.** Related to this effort are informational pieces that can be written and submitted to newspapers. Articles on a new teaching aid or technique—such as "What are those...math manipulatives or toys?"—can be written and then submitted to an editor. It is more difficult to get an editor to commit space for this type of article, but the value of publication is enormous.

As the leader in your school system, you must repeatedly articulate the value of writing these communications pieces to your staff, students, board members, parents, and other support groups. The importance of the task must be highlighted and rewarded. The importance of *timeliness* in this activity must also be emphasized. A letter to the editor must be written when it is needed, not after the fact. Today's news may be forgotten next week if someone does not capture the moment, write a letter, and submit it to the editor.

**District newsletters.** The limited funds at your disposal should be judiciously spent. One of the best allocations might be for publishing a district newsletter—a solid, fact-filled, professional way to get your message to target audiences on a regular basis. Desktop publishing programs are available at most schools, so the newsletters can look great as well.

With the district newsletter, you can tell your many customers your school's mission, goals, and objectives; current and future school activities; what school events they can attend; how you can help them; and how they can help you. This newsletter is one of the best ways to build relationships with key customer segments.

**Pictures tell the story best.** When a reporter comes to school to cover a story, ask if a photographer can be sent, too. If the photographer takes pictures and some appear with the article, consider buying the photos from the newspaper for your school photo file. These photos can be used in future publicity pieces; framed and hung in the school for a "feel-good" display; and given to staff, students, and parents as keepsakes.

Your school system should also designate your own school photographer. This person should receive a nominal budget and attend special school events and activities where photographs would help convey the message. The school photographer should work closely with the EdMarketing Coordinator.

The school photographer could make his or her photo file available to newspapers when a reporter is researching a story or the school submits an article for publication. Make it easy for the newspaper to showcase your school system in whatever way you can.

Ironically, many school systems do not consider taking pictures of special events—a major publicity opportunity—even though they know the value of a picture. This is a great loss because people will often look only at pictures and not read the copy! Even though a photo can tell a story instantly, many schools consider photography to be a frill instead of a necessary, integral way to promote their schools.

The photographs on the following pages (and the wonderful headlines that accompany them) illustrate the medium's ability to send clear, positive

*HOW SMART SCHOOLS GET AND KEEP COMMUNITY SUPPORT*

messages about public education. No text is needed. Feelings are immediately conveyed to the viewer.

## READING TOGETHER

## BREAKING DOWN BARRIERS

120

*Marketing Communication Strategies*

# FIRST DAY OF KINDERGARTEN

**Keep a "clip file" of any newspaper coverage that you get.** Positive or negative, these clippings will be useful in the future and can serve as a springboard for your own communication pieces. Newspaper clippings should be collected on any person affiliated with your school system and on any program, school, or school district. When in doubt, clip it out.

## Strategy #8: Develop Your Marketing Communications with Senior Citizens in Mind

Many public schools feel that the elderly are their worst enemy because they are often unwilling to support public education in local budgets due to their fixed incomes and the perception that public education no longer benefits them. Such reluctance will be the demographic reality, however, and will increase in significance for decades to come as the 76 million Baby Boomers grow older and begin focusing on their retirement needs. School systems need to develop all of their marketing communications with the senior citizen market in mind if they want to ensure strong community support in the future.

Because certain physical and psychological changes associated with aging may affect a senior citizen's ability to understand your marketing communications, you may want to apply the following guidelines:

1. **Keep the message as simple and concrete as possible.** Think about what you really need to say to convey your message. Boil it down, and then boil it down again.

2. **Repeat the message.** Don't change it. Once the message is delivered, it should be repeatedly delivered in the same way. Familiarity will make the message easier to assimilate.

3. **Favor print media over TV and radio.** As persons age, the speed with which they can process information changes and can vary widely. Print media provides an unlimited time for comprehension so readers can process the information at their own pace.

4. **Make full use of context.** The more pleasant the context (wedding, birth, graduation, birthday), the easier the message will be to remember.

## Summary

Marketing communications is a discipline. It should not be left to chance or done halfheartedly or irregularly. If it is to have a positive effect for a school system, there has to be a *plan* for implementation, actual *implementation* in a systematic and deliberate way, and then *evaluation* of the implementation.

DeLapp and Smith (1991) conclude that "in today's fast paced information age, schools have to compete for public attention. A carefully developed communications plan can help position your school in the public marketplace of information [and] improve your image and community support."

In the final analysis, isn't that what we all want?

**CHAPTER 10**

# PASSING A SCHOOL REFERENDUM: A SAVVY MIX OF POLITICS AND MARKETING

School boards, educators, and concerned parents find themselves increasingly dependent on the outcomes of referenda to maintain the quality of academic programs. The growing need for school building construction or renovation and swelling enrollments have led to fierce debates over school budgets in communities throughout the U.S. Ultimately, the public determines the scope of local education programs through the ballot box.

Building the voter support needed to pass a bond or budget referenda presents a worrisome challenge for many school systems. And well it should—most are unprepared to develop the political power and marketing strategies necessary to mount a successful electoral campaign. This chapter focuses on the concepts and strategies smart schools need to understand and use when proposing a school referendum.

## Winners and Losers

In spite of the chilly political climate, many communities have passed educational referenda. What distinguishes them from those communities that fail to get a bond issue accepted or referendum passed?

1. **Winners know that an educational referendum is a political campaign.** Because a referendum decides the distribution of limited funds within the community, it involves all of a community's sources of power—government, business, citizen groups, the media—and is therefore highly political.

According to Etheredge (1987), winners understand the political nature of their task. Theirs is a competitive contest calling for strategy and a well-orchestrated campaign. They make it their business to learn the sophisticated rules of the electioneering game. Their campaigns are characterized by well-conceived political strategy and organization.

To be effective, supporters of public education need to *run their referendum according to the principles of electioneering and voting behavior.* Electoral success is determined not only by what needs to be said, but also by how it is said, to whom it is said, and when it is said. Doing this well requires planning, organization, communication, funding, and—most importantly—time.

2. **Winners know that a successful referendum relies on the school system's marketing efforts to date.** Winners know that much of the support or opposition *is formulated well in advance of the campaign.* The school system's marketing efforts are crucial:

- Have the schools adequately involved the community in their programs?
- Do teachers and staff take an active role in community organizations and events?
- Does the community know how well its schools perform in relation to comparable schools in the state?

The school system that has made an investment in marketing will have a far easier time collecting its dividend on election day.

## WINNING STRATEGIES

A new school. A modernized media center. A foreign language program. All of these represent new products which must be "sold" in the marketplace—the community. Whether there is sufficient demand to "buy" these products might ultimately be determined by a referendum. The following competitive strategies can make the difference.

**Don't educate the voters during the campaign.** This principle is based on assumptions of voting behavior and the nature of a campaign. Fishel (1987) states that "if your goal is to change attitudes, you have your work cut out for you. Generally, a campaign is not the place to do this."

First, *how a person votes is often determined by existing attitudes*. The perceived quality of local public education and the image of the school will influence a vote for or against the initiative.

Second, *voters tend to decide how they will vote early in a campaign*. Many decide before the referendum is even announced. Thus, voter opinion remains relatively constant during a campaign.

Third, *the issues introduced by an educational referendum are complicated*. The campaign does not allow sufficient time to present all of the important aspects of the referendum. Faucheux (1993) notes that "complexity scares voters. Complex propositions are rarely passed by selling specifics."

**Use a two-phased approach: Education and Campaign.** The **education phase** begins as early as two years before the election. During this time, school officials and volunteers *identify the nature and extent of the issues that their system will have to address in the future* through long-range planning studies of enrollments, programs, and facilities.

It is equally important *to establish public recognition of the issues that the school system is facing (and their legitimacy) and to begin attracting community support for the potential recommended action*. The educational phase should create a public forum through which all of an issue's aspects can be discussed and better understood without pressing time constraints.

The **campaign phase** involves activities intended *to identify supporters, reinforce their commitment, and ensure they vote*. Campaign planning should begin 9 months to a year before the referendum. The planning should result in a written campaign plan at least 3 months before the referendum. The detailed work of building an organization, acquiring resources, and initiating voter contact programs should begin about 3 months before the referendum.

In most states, school officials are prohibited both from campaigning for the passage of a school bond issue and spending public funds on the campaign. While school officials can make factual presentations to the public concerning the bond issue, they are prevented from urging the electorate to "Vote Yes." Typically, *ad hoc* citizens committees or legally established political action committees are formed to carry out the campaign phase, which includes planning, communications, and fund-raising.

## PHASE 1: EDUCATING THE VOTER

**Step 1. Determine the school system's mission, goals, and objectives** by formulating a long-range strategic plan. The plan should affirm the system's purpose and document its goals for programming, physical facilities, staff development, community involvement, and other areas over the next 5 to 10 years.

*The school system must identify the gap between those future objectives and the system's present status.* By establishing need, the strategic plan becomes the foundation for future budget and capital initiatives. A comprehensive plan should include the following:

***Demographic trends.*** Demographic trend analysis should firmly establish the extent of projected needs. By doing its demographic homework, the school system can project enrollments for 5 to 10 years. The following demographic indicators can affect school enrollments and should be examined:

- Number of births to community residents
- Projected number of births based on age-specific fertility rates
- Population projections
- Ratio of kindergarten enrollments to actual births
- Number and type of housing units constructed
- Number and type of building lots approved
- Household composition of new housing units
- Location of new and approved housing units

***Programmatic trends.*** Trend analysis will help school systems determine the extent to which they will have to add, modify, or discontinue programs. The many benefits of this proactive process include the opportunity to help the public understand the issues local schools will face and the financial implications these issues may represent to the community.

***A facilities master plan.*** A comprehensive plan will justify the school system's long-term needs from both a facility and programmatic perspective, identify options for meeting them, and determine the costs and timetable for action. The plan should include:

- The potential options for addressing projected need for additional space to meet changes in enrollments and/or curriculum,
- The potential options for additional space to address programmatic inequities between schools, and
- The capital improvements required to remedy deteriorating conditions and to comply with building code requirements.

**Step 2. Analyze system strengths and weaknesses.** Employee satisfaction and program performance should be assessed before launching a referendum.

*Support and involvement of school employees are critical.* Employee satisfaction influences attitudes that can either promote or undercut internal support for a future educational initiative. Employee feedback should be sought on a regular basis, and action should be taken to resolve identified problems. Lack of employee involvement could critically limit the campaign's human resources, affect their commitment to vote, and negatively influence how family members and friends perceive the referendum.

*Effectiveness of school programs also plays a meaningful role.* School systems which regularly evaluate their programs, as recommended in Chapter 7, create additional opportunities for conveying a persuasive campaign message. A system that can promote high standardized test scores or exemplary academic programs, for example, maximizes its chances for a positive response when it has to ask taxpayers to vote for a budget increase.

**Step 3. Identify and assess external threats and opportunities.** The external environment should be studied long before school officials begin to formulate the referendum or plan campaign strategy. What taxpayers want, what they are willing to support, and how political and economic conditions affect them are key considerations. The answers to these and similar questions will help school officials decide what to do as well as when and how to do it. Three parts of the external environment should be considered:

*The public.* Community taxpayers, businesses, human service and religious organizations, civic groups, etc.

*The opposition and competition.* The segment of the public most likely to oppose requests for increased education expenditures and any governmental entities which may be seeking increased public funding.

***The macroenvironment.*** The broad social, economic, and political forces potentially influencing community perceptions of the school system's need for increased funding.

## The Public

There are two methods for obtaining information on the public which can be invaluable to referendum planning. The *community study* (discussed in Chapter 4) helps school officials understand how the public perceives the system's performance. The *issue survey* solicits public opinion on issues related to referendum planning and is most useful when conducted 8 to 12 months before the referendum. The issue survey should be designed to answer 2 major questions:

**What projects or programs is the community willing to support?** It is critical to determine if the majority of voters will support the school system when its needs are stated in proposals. For example, school officials may believe it is important to limit elementary classroom sizes to 25 pupils to enhance learning. Will taxpayers vote for the budget increase to hire the additional teacher needed to maintain that ratio? If space is unavailable, will they support a bond issue to purchase portable classrooms?

**What is the community willing to pay to support those projects or programs?** By identifying acceptable tax rates, school officials can structure a proposal with a higher potential for passage. For example, although most voters favor renovating several schools, the issue survey indicated that the tax rate voters are willing to accept is considerably less than the options require. The survey has pinpointed the questions school officials need to answer before going to referendum. Do they lower their expectations to what is politically feasible? Do they eliminate certain components that have less voter appeal? Or do they spend more time in the education phase convincing voters that the costlier option is the best solution?

Given the importance of the issue survey to formulating a sellable bond proposal, random sampling techniques must be incorporated. The group of respondents should match the demographic composition of the voting community.

## The Opposition and Competition

**The opposition.** Strong, organized opposition is often the primary factor in lost referenda. Unfortunately, serious consideration of the opposition often comes only after it has publicized arguments that were not considered and convinced once-sympathetic voters to oppose the referendum.

Although organized opposition usually does not materialize until a campaign begins, schools can use the issue survey to collect a considerable amount of information about it before establishing the referendum question. The survey should determine answers to these questions:

- Who opposes this project(s)/budget?
- Why do they oppose it?
- What would they support?
- How likely is the opposition to become organized?
- How strong is the opposition likely to be?

Assessment is particularly valuable when combined with demographic information, such as age and voting history. For example, many parents of secondary school students may not support any proposal increasing property taxes since they see no immediate benefits for their families. On the other hand, senior citizens who have grandchildren in the schools may support some options.

School officials gain several strategic advantages by collecting information on their opposition before establishing the referendum question. First, they can structure their proposal to neutralize the opponents' arguments. Second, they can plan their communication program with accuracy. Third, they can minimize the potential for surprises by predicting their opponents' arguments, sources of support, and weaknesses.

**The competition.** Other public agencies and services often compete for a greater share of limited public funds to expand services and implement programs. Thus, school officials need to assess the community's priorities for its tax dollars. For example, do taxpayers feel that police or fire protection needs to be expanded? If so, they may support budget requests for more personnel, training, or equipment.

Detecting the emergence of these or other competing demands on public funds is an important task for school officials presenting a referendum. Whenever the public is forced to choose how its tax dollars will be spent, there will be conflicting values and competition. School officials who recognize this will use the issue survey to determine the extent of their competition and how it may affect a referendum. They will also meet with community leaders to discuss future community needs.

## The Macroenvironment

In assessing threats to their strategic plans, school officials must consider environmental forces affecting the community. Voter attitudes about school referenda can be influenced by trends and events over which the community has little or no control. Understanding how the external environment may impact an upcoming referendum will help school officials develop effective strategies.

School systems can benefit from the three-step approach of environmental scanning with a minimal investment of time and resources. The first step is to identify the external forces that may influence a referendum. Figure 10-1 may help you determine what should be examined. If knowing more about an environmental factor will help you make decisions, you should identify and collect data on that factor.

### Figure 10-1. ENVIRONMENTAL FACTORS

| | |
|---|---|
| *Demography* | Migration patterns |
| | Population projections |
| *Household/ family income* | Changes in median household income |
| | Incidence of delinquent tax payments |
| *Legal/political* | Legislation affecting funding to municipalities |
| | Tax and/or millrate increases |
| *Economic/ labor force* | Business openings/closings |
| | Business relocations |
| | Inflation rate |
| | Interest rates on mortgages, loans, and credit |
| | Layoffs |
| | Unemployment rate |
| *Transportation* | Changes in commuting patterns |

The second step is to collect information on relevant factors. The many information sources readily accessible to school officials may include census data, daily newspapers, educational newsletters and journals, and state and regional planning reports. City planning, housing, and tax collection departments maintain data that can be very helpful in tracking environmental trends in the community.

The third step is to analyze the data and determine how these environmental factors may affect a possible referendum. Focus on the events and trends that may influence voter attitudes and perceptions and then identify how each highlighted event or trend might affect referendum strategy.

**Step 4. Determine the referendum plan.** School officials must use what they learn in the first three steps to determine the content of the referendum plan. The plan establishes how project or program objectives will be met and funded by the referendum. There are four key elements of a referendum plan.

*Structure.* What should the components be? Should the building referendum involve new construction, renovation/expansion of existing facilities, or be limited to the provision of transitional facilities (i.e., portable classrooms)?

*Scope.* How extensive should the plan be? Should the new foreign language program be demonstrated only at the 8th-grade level or be incorporated throughout all the middle grades?

*Cost.* What are the feasible minimum and maximum cost ranges for the proposal?

*Timing.* When is the most favorable time for holding a referendum? The least favorable? Should the referendum be pursued now or would the chance for approval be improved by a delay?

After determining the referendum plan, school officials can begin the tasks required to bring a final plan to referendum by developing a detailed proposal that meets educational goals and specifications and includes a justifiable budget. Proponents should also begin discussing the strategy that will ensure plan approval.

**Step 5. Develop the core political strategy.** As the unifying structure of the entire campaign, the core political strategy guides all campaign decisions, including political activities, resource requirements, and timetables. This step determines what must be done to win and involves making decisions on three essential components:

- The specific *target groups* or voter segments needed to win the referendum,
- The *message* that will be communicated to those target groups, and
- The *marketing mix* or communications tools that will be used to convey the message.

Making these decisions will help proponents avoid the mistake of trying to do everything, for everybody, everywhere. According to Napolitan (1987), "strategy is the single most important factor in a political campaign. The right strategy can survive a mediocre campaign, but even a brilliant campaign is likely to fail if the strategy is wrong."

# PHASE 2: THE CAMPAIGN

## Strategic Decision #1
*Identify target groups and assess their electoral strength.*

Which target groups or voter segments are most likely to support the referendum and do they represent the electoral strength (in numbers of votes) needed to win? Answers to these questions provide the foundation for campaign strategy. With this information, proponents can confidently and effectively "target" their supporters with the campaign message and ensure they vote. The two methods used to segment the electorate are demographic targeting and electoral targeting.

**Demographic targeting** involves dividing the community's voters into different groups based on characteristics and then selecting the groups with the most potential for supporting a pro-education issue. Proponents should also identify the members of the target groups (i.e., their names, addresses, and telephone numbers) and obtain mailing lists when possible. Target groups could include parents of students, parents of preschoolers, newlyweds, grandparents of preschoolers and students, and alumni who are college students. Proponents must examine their own communities to determine if there are additional groups that may be potential supporters.

Once the target groups have been selected, **electoral targeting** is used to establish the relative importance of each group to the campaign by determining its electoral strength. This is done by comparing lists for each target group with local voter registration files and election records to determine if the member (1) is a registered voter, (2) votes in general elections, (3) and votes in referenda.

**The gold ring: 50% plus 1.** This information leads to the most important consideration: Is the electoral strength of the target groups enough to win the referendum? To determine the answer, estimate the overall vote total by reviewing the turnout of previous referenda and making adjustments for circumstances which may affect the turnout for the upcoming referendum. Then estimate the number of votes needed to win the referendum by dividing the projected vote total in half and adding one vote.

Assessing electoral strength early in a campaign gives education proponents the opportunity to adjust campaign planning when it can make a difference. They may need to identify other potentially supportive groups or sponsor a voter registration drive to increase the strength of their existing target groups.

(As a note, education proponents must pay attention to state and local mandates which may require minimum levels of voter participation and/or a positive vote greater than 50% plus 1—*in order for the outcome to be binding*. Regardless, the strategy remains. You must assess the electoral strength of the target groups—relative to the threshold for victory.)

## Strategic Decision #2
*Design an effective campaign message.*

An effective message will reinforce the convictions of a committed supporter and persuade an undecided voter that the pro-education position merits his or her support. Designing an effective message should include the following considerations:

> *Each statement should be evaluated in light of how it might be read by various non-parent populations.... Each statement should be questioned to avoid potential misunderstandings. Each statement should be evaluated to avoid educational or legal jargon. Each document should be as concise and readable as possible. (Senden, 1993)*

One critical part of message design is determining how the message will be positioned (as discussed in Chapter 5). Positioning can be used to create "the right message" by concentrating "on the perceptions of the prospect [voter] rather than on the attributes of the product [referendum]" (Ries and Trout, 1986). An effectively positioned message will:

- Communicate the strengths of the pro-education issue in a way that potential supporters understand and value,
- Clearly differentiate the pro-education issue from the position of the opposition, and
- Be presented in a way that helps voters readily perceive the difference between the two positions.

1. **Find out what the voters think.** Voter attitudes and perceptions greatly influence how the message is received. Before asserting why proposal X is the best alternative, you must first understand reality as defined by the community's voters (Price, 1990). Community surveys and issue surveys will provide the information needed to identify general attitudes and should also be reviewed to determine the:

- Perceptions of education generally and the performance of the local school system in particular.
- Attitudes toward the Board of Education, administration, and teaching staff.
- Types of projects voters are willing to support.
- Amount of additional tax expenditures voters are willing to accept.

2. **Determine what the voters want to know.** This second step is perhaps the most important, and the most difficult, because the information selected will be the basis on which many voters, particularly the undecided, will make their decision.

First, proponents must make every effort to determine what is relevant to the voters they want to persuade. Second, proponents should focus the message on the questions for which a majority of voters has expressed interest or concern.

Before making any decision on message content, proponents should identify the three or four most prominent issues raised by the voters. For each issue, choose the key facts which best reflect the pro-education position and directly address voter concerns.

The following typical questions asked by voters during a referendum (Flores and Lake, 1990) should provide some guidance to proponents:

- Why do we need to do anything?
- Why is this the best solution?
- How much is this going to cost me?
- What benefit will I receive for supporting this issue?

3. **Find out what the opposition is saying.** Another important aspect of effective communications is what Kotler and Andreasen (1991) call a "differentiated market position." The message must be presented in a way that ensures voters will perceive a real difference between the pro-education position and that of the opposition. To do this, evaluate the opposition's position by asking:

- What is their assessment of the problem?
- What are their major disagreements with the pro-education proposal?
- What are they proposing as an alternative?

Ries and Trout (1986) stress that "the competitor's position is just as important as your own. Sometimes more important." Competitive intelligence can be used to formulate a message that not only promotes the benefits of the pro-education position but also "repositions the opposition" by presenting the pro-education message in a way that undermines the main points of the opposition. Listed below are several positions that can accomplish this.

- The opposition has been *unreasonable* in its refusal to support any of the proposed options despite the community's general agreement that a problem exists.
- The opposition has demonstrated *incompetence* through its inability to develop options that realistically address the problem.

4. **Generate a campaign message for target voters.** If the preceding steps have been followed, the campaign message for targeted voters will be

fairly obvious. Two points may express the desired merits of the pro-education proposal. The third point may position the proposal favorably against the alternative espoused by the opposition. To distill the available information into the two or three major points, practice three principles.

***KISS (keep it simple, stupid!).*** The points being communicated must be concise and phrased in easily understood language. (See the campaign advertisements reproduced on pages 93-97.)

***Consistency.*** Never change your message or positioning strategy during the campaign. The strength of the message must not be diluted by trying to respond to issues not critical to target voters or on rebutting the opposition.

***Repetition.*** The impact of positioning is cumulative. Even targeted voters will need to hear the message many times in order for it to influence their voting behavior.

## Strategic Decision #3
*Determine the mix of tools needed to communicate the campaign message.*

This difficult decision is made even harder by the limited resources of many referendum campaigns. Careful planning is required since the considerations include not only *what tools to use,* but also *where and when to use them.* Choosing the best "communications mix" should depend on the communications objectives, available resources, and available communications tools.

The first two questions below are very important and should be answered before choosing individual communications tools.

1. **What are we trying to achieve?** Communications objectives should be clearly established and based on the following information:

- The number of target voters needed to win the referendum.
- The location of target voters...geographically, demographically, psychographically.
- The message(s) that should be communicated to them.

2. **What resources are available?** Available campaign resources should be evaluated in terms of campaign funding and volunteers.

***Campaign funding.*** One question every pro-education campaign has to consider is whether or not to raise funds. Two factors can provide guidance in deciding the funding issue—the community tradition on referendum spending and the perceived level of difficulty in achieving the communications objectives.

Communities accustomed to low-key, low-budget referenda will certainly frown on a well-financed campaign and its communications activities. Conversely, pro-education campaign spending may not be an issue in communities which have previously experienced high-profile elections or referenda.

The difficulties presented by the communications objectives may override the community's attitude toward campaign spending. *The greater the expectations of what communications needs to achieve, the greater the problems resulting from a limited campaign budget.* The need for a campaign budget will increase commensurately if some or all the following factors are present:

- A sizable bond issue or budget request.
- A large number of registered voters within the district.
- Stringent local requirements for passing a referendum (i.e., two-thirds majority).
- A sizable school district (i.e., several towns spread over a large geographic area).
- An older electorate (i.e., a large number of households without children in the school system).
- Previous electoral defeats.
- The prevalence of recent bond issues and tax increases.
- Recent reevaluation of property.
- Negative public attitudes toward education and/or the local school system or Board of Education.

The budget, or lack thereof, will determine the extent to which certain communications tools can be used. For example, direct mail is a very effective tool, but it is relatively expensive and requires repetition. On the other hand, free media coverage can reach voters at a very low cost, but the campaign loses control over how and to whom its message is communicated.

***Volunteers.*** The importance of volunteers should not be underestimated. Every communications tool requires volunteer services. Some tools, such as literature drops and telephone banks, call for a substantial number of volunteers. The extent to which organizers can successfully recruit volunteers will have a direct effect on the type of communications tools a campaign can use.

3. **Which types of communications tools should we use?** Communications tools are the means through which organizers send their campaign message to target groups of potential supporters. Pro-education organizers have nine primary communications tools at their disposal (see the Appendix), which vary in their costs (in dollars and human resources), ability to communicate information, and potential number of voters they are capable of reaching.

Deciding how to allocate limited resources among the selected communications tools can only be done by evaluating each tool in relationship to the campaign's communications objectives and available resources. Completing Table 10-1 (on the next page) will help organizers design and evaluate different mixes of communications tools. A review of Chapter 8 will help organizers evaluate other options.

# SUMMARY

Although there is no secret formula for winning a referendum, two elements will increase the potential for electoral victory if they are effectively applied. This chapter has focused on the first element—planning.

Yet this chapter cannot end without acknowledging the other essential campaign element—*organizing*. Roger Ailes, the mastermind of several winning presidential campaigns, has stated that "politics is execution." Planning alone will not win a referendum; organization is also necessary for success.

Although campaign planning is hard work, campaign organizing is even harder. Even so, the most impressive campaign plan is nothing more than a document until it is put into action. Once the strategy is formulated, *use it*.

The execution of an effective strategy will persuade voters and inspire them to go to the polls. If education supporters invest the time and effort required to plan, organize, and implement their referendum campaign, they have every reason to expect electoral victory.

## Table 10-1.
## Worksheet for Evaluating Communications Tools

**Total Campaign Budget:**

**Total Number of Volunteers:**

| Resource Requirements | | | Message Impact | | | |
|---|---|---|---|---|---|---|
| Communications Tool | Dollar Cost | Volunteers Needed | Type of Contact | Amount of Contact | Type of Information | Potential Number of Voters Reached |
| | | | | | | |

CHAPTER 11

# SMART SCHOOLS CAN MEET THE CHALLENGES OF THE FUTURE

When school systems embrace a marketing orientation by placing the customer first and religiously employing the strategies outlined in this book, they will enjoy an improved public image, have happier employees and, most important, gain the community support they need to meet the formidable challenges of the future.

And the future will be particularly challenging for public schools. As they strive to provide needed programs, many of them mandated by law, schools will face a voting community of customers increasingly reluctant to fund something they believe does not provide benefits commensurate with their tax investment.

The demographic trends affecting public education further complicate the situation and will have a tremendous impact in the future. **There is a shrinking market of public education users (school-aged children) and a growing market of non-users (empty nesters and senior citizens).**

From 1990 to 2000,

- There will be a 6% decline in the number of children under age 5,
- There will be a 14% increase in the number of 55- to 64-year-olds, and
- There will be a 26% increase of those over 65 years old.

Nevertheless, *smart schools* will turn these challenges into opportunities. These leaders will be known for the 10 characteristics that all *smart schools* possess. The new way of thinking—EdMarketing—will be integrated into everyday school life to help schools meet the challenges they will face in the tough years ahead.

## 10 Characteristics of Smart Schools

1. **Capturing and retaining community support will be a primary goal** that is established in strategic long-range plans.

2. **"Quality" will be a priority.** Quality programs and services will be achieved through constant innovation and improvement. Program evaluations will be used to showcase quality.

3. **Customer input will be solicited** for decision-making, idea generation, and overall improvement. Complaints will be solicited and acted upon, and there will be no arguing with customers.

4. **A climate of customer orientation will prevail.** Parents will have an open invitation to visit at any time. Points of interaction with the customer will be identified and reviewed to make each better. Policies and procedures will be developed from a customer's point of view.

5. **Employees will be recruited, hired, evaluated positively, and rewarded if they display a customer orientation.** Training in this area will be a part of professional development.

6. **Employee satisfaction will be assessed** on a regular basis, and the findings will be taken seriously and acted upon.

7. **Demographics will be monitored faithfully.** Birth rates, in-migration, new housing, family structures, age, and ethnic composition of markets will be tabulated and analyzed in terms of their effect on the school system.

8. **Information will be issued regularly,** systematically, and professionally throughout the school year. If appropriate, communications will be multilingual. Database marketing will be used to develop communication channels and to build relationships.

9. **The school grounds and buildings will be neat, pleasant, accessible and welcoming.** The community will attend special events at the schools, and the media will cover and photograph these events.

10. **Budget time will be less painful.**

## APPENDIX

# CAMPAIGN COMMUNICATIONS TOOLS

| Communications Tools | Definition |
| --- | --- |
| 1. Paid advertising—print and broadcast media | Information and/or notices placed in print and broadcast media in the form of a paid political announcement, including newspapers, radio, and television. |
| 2. Paid advertising—outdoor media | Information and/or notices placed in outdoor advertising media in the form of a paid political announcement, including bilboards, yard signs, and bumper stickers. |
| 3. Free media | Information presented as news in print and broadcast media, placed as a result of a public announcement or event planned by the campaign. These include press conferences, press releases, and special events. |

## Campaign Communications Tools

| Characteristics | Resource Requirements |
|---|---|
| • Impersonal contact with voters<br>• Effectiveness contingent on repeated contacts<br>• Print media allows for detailed information; TV and radio usually communicate general information<br>• Can reach large numbers of voters<br>• Low degree of control over type of voters reached; contact includes both nonsupporters and nonvoters<br>• Allows for high degree of control over message design<br>• Can be persuasive and dramatic | • Requires substantial campaign budget<br>• Few volunteers needed<br>• Requires communications consultant or volunteers with communications experience |
| • Impersonal contact with voters<br>• Effectiveness contingent on saturation of placement<br>• Capacity to convey information is very low—at best, the campaign theme will be conveyed<br>• Can reach large number of voters<br>• Low degree of control over type of voter reached—contact reaches both nonsupporters and nonvoters | • Requires substantial campaign budget<br>• Requires few volunteers |
| • Impersonal contact with voters<br>• Can involve either one-time or repeated contact<br>• Usually involves communication of detailed information<br>• High degree of credibility—perceived as "real" news<br>• Can reach large numbers of voters<br>• Low degree of control over type of voters reached<br>• Lower degree of control over message communicated than through paid advertising | • Low financial cost<br>• Few volunteers required<br>• Requires communications consultant or volunteers with communications experience |

*(Continued)*

| Communications Tools | Definition |
| --- | --- |
| 4. Direct mail | The mailing of campaign literature to individuals' homes, frequently in bulk format. The mailing is usually targeted to households based on their selected characteristics and drawn from compiled mailing lists. |
| 5. Telephone banks | Personal telephone calls made by teams of volunteers, frequently in central locations, to the electorate to elicit and identify their support, answer questions, and remind them to vote. Calls are usually targeted to households based on their selected characteristics. |
| 6. Literature drops | The direct distribution of campaign literature to individuals' homes by teams of volunteers walking through targeted neighborhoods. |

## Campaign Communications Tools

| Characteristics | Resource Requirements |
|---|---|
| • Impersonal contact with voters<br>• Effectiveness greatly increased by repeated contacts<br>• Detailed information can be communicated<br>• High degree of control over type of voters reached (can target potential supporters)<br>• High degree of control over message design<br>• Can be very persuasive | • Requires considerable financial resources (including production and mailing costs)<br>• Requires volunteers to prepare mailing (fewer numbers than telephone banks and literature drops)<br>• Requires communications consultant or volunteers with communications experience |
| • Personal contact with voters<br>• Usually involves one-time contact (persuasion) and follow-up contact (reminder to vote)<br>• General information is communicated<br>• Reaches fewer voters than advertising<br>• High degree of control over type of voter reached (can target potential supporters)<br>• High degree of control over message design<br>• Can be very persuasive | • Low financial costs, if in-kind contributions are made<br>• Requires large numbers of volunteers<br>• Requires facilities with multiple telephone lines |
| • Impersonal contact with voters<br>• One-time contact (unless part of a larger direct-mail or neighborhood walk strategy)<br>• Detailed information can be communicated<br>• High degree of control over type of voters reached (can target potential supporters in important areas)<br>• Generally reaches fewer numbers of targeted voters compared to other tools | • Low financial cost<br>• Requires large numbers of volunteers<br>• Requires considerable planning and volunteer coordination |

*(Continued)*

| Communications Tools | Definition |
|---|---|
| 7. Neighborhood walk and talk | Face-to-face contact with voters at their homes by teams of volunteers walking through targeted neighborhoods to elicit and identify voter support and answer questions. |
| 8. Public speaking | Presentations made to business and civic groups, PTOs/PTAs, and coffee klatch groups to provide them with information about the referendum and to elicit their support. The presentations are frequently made by persons with high visibility within the community. |
| 9. Letters to the editor | Letters written to the editors of print media to express support of the referendum issue. |

## Campaign Communications Tools

| Characteristics | Resource Requirements |
|---|---|
| • Highly personal contact<br>• One-time contact (persuasion)<br>• General information is communicated (with a leave-behind brochure containing detailed information)<br>• High degree of control over type of voters reached (can target potential supporters in important areas)<br>• Fewer numbers of potential voters reached compared to other tools<br>• Provides visual show of volunteer commitment and support<br>• Can be very persuasive | • Low financial costs<br>• Requires large numbers of volunteers<br>• Requires considerable planning and volunteer coordination |
| • Highly personal contact (face to face)<br>• One-time contact<br>• Detailed information is communicated<br>• Fewer members of potential supporters reached compared to other tools<br>• Lower degree of control over type of voter reached (includes nonsupporters and nonvoters)<br>• High degree of control over message design<br>• Can be very persuasive | • Low financial costs<br>• Few volunteers needed<br>• Requires trained volunteers who are comfortable speaking to the public |
| • Impersonal contact with voters<br>• Effectiveness greatly increased by repeated contact (as part of letter-writing campaign) and by participation of highly visible members of the community<br>• Detailed information can be communicated<br>• High degree of credibility—perceived as "real" news<br>• Can reach large numbers of voters<br>• Low degree of control over type of voters reached<br>• High degree of control over message design<br>• Can be persuasive | • Requires no financial cost<br>• Requires few volunteers<br>• Requires recruitment of writers, technical assistance, and coordination of message design |

# REFERENCES AND RESOURCES

Ambry, M.K. (1989). *Almanac of Consumer Markets.* Ithaca, NY: American Demographics Press.

American Association of School Administrators (1992). *Schoolhouse in the Red.* Arlington, VA.

Ames, J.V. (1991). Getting the word out. *Thrust for Educational Leadership,* May-June, 12-14.

Armistead, L. (1989). A four step process for school public relations. *NASSP Bulletin,* January, 6-13.

Blumenthal, R. (1991). Just do it isn't enough. *Thrust for Educational Leadership,* June, 15-17.

Bogue, D.J. (1969). *Principles of Demography.* New York: John Wiley and Sons, 1.

Cannon, C.L., & Barnham, F.E. (1993). Are you and your public polls far apart? *The Executive Educator,* October, 41-42.

Carey, J. (1993). Building a strong public image of yourself. *Thrust for Educational Leadership,* September, 12-15.

Carroll, S.R. (1992). The employee as a marketing tool. *Employers Digest,* December, 1.

Cetron, M.J., & Gayle, M.E. (1990). Educational renaissance: 43 trends for U.S. schools. *The Futurist,* September-October, 33-40.

Chew, K., et al. (1991). Who cares about public schools? *American Demographics,* May, 38-39.

Conyers, J.G. (1989). We turned to Madison Avenue for tips on selling our $64 million bond issue. *The American School Board Journal,* October, 27-28.

Crispell, D. (1991). Classrooms crowded? Fire the school board. *American Demographics,* April, 13.

Cutler, B. (1990). Enlightened orphans. *American Demographics,* March, 16.

DeLapp, T., & Smith, D. (1991). Schools in the spotlight. *Thrust for Educational Leadership,* May-June, 8-11.

Deutsch, C.H. (1990). Asking workers what they think. *New York Times,* April 22, 34.

Edmondson, B. (1989). *Cornering the Children's Market.* Ithaca, NY: American Demographics Press.

Education Writers Association (1989). *Wolves at the Schoolhouse Door.* Washington, D.C.

Elam, S. (1993). 25th annual Gallup poll of the public attitude toward the public school. *Phi Delta Kappan,* October, 138-152.

Etheredge, F. (1987). *School Boards and the Ballot Box.* Alexandria, VA: National School Boards Association.

Faucheux, R. (1993). The referendum game. *Campaigns and Elections,* August, 47-48.

Feistritzer, C.E. (1987). Schools learn a lesson. *American Demographics,* November, 42-43.

Fishel, M. (1987). Strategic thinking and the low budget campaign. *Campaigns and Elections,* January-February, 20-24.

Flores, R., & Lake, S. (1990). Election success story. *Thrust for Educational Leadership,* September, 23-26.

Franchese, P.A. (1989). *Trends and Opportunities in the Children's Market.* Ithaca, NY: American Demographics Press.

Henderson, A.T. (1986). *Beyond the Bake Sale: An Educators Guide to Working with Parents.* Columbia, MD: National Committee for Citizens in Education.

Henderson, E.H. (1990). Cast a wide net. *The American School Board Journal*, March, 38-39.

Hines, R.W. (1993). Principal starts with PR. *Principal*, January, 45-46.

Houston, P.D. (1993). Telling the truth about today's schools. *Thrust for Educational Leadership*, September, 8-11.

Howlett, P. (1993). People power: Strategies for shaping public opinion. *The American School Board Journal*, March, 50-51.

Issac, S., & Michael, W.B. (1981). *Handbook of Research and Evaluation*. Second Edition. San Diego, CA: EDITS.

Jackson, R. (1988). Most neglected market: Your own employees. *Marketing News*, November 7, 4.

Kenner, L., & Gribbin, R. (1992). Community involvement: Linking parents and non-parents. *Principal*, November, 26-27.

Kotler, P. (1975). *Marketing for Non-Profit Organizations*. Englewoods Cliff, NJ: Prentice Hall.

Kotler, P., & Andreasen, A. (1991). *Strategic Marketing for Non-profit Organizations*. Englewoods Cliff, NJ: Prentice Hall.

Kudlacek, B. (1989). Special interest groups: Friends or foes? *NASSP Bulletin*, January, 29-32.

Leslie, K. (1989). Administrators must consider and improve teacher satisfaction. *NASSP Bulletin*, January, 19-22.

Lindle, J. (1989). Market analysis identifies community and school goals. *NASSP Bulletin*, November, 62-66.

Lyons, C. (1990). Getting the ink. *The American School Board Journal*, November, 37.

May, P.R. (1990). Junk is in the eye of the beholder. *Marketing News*, February 5, 16.

Mijares, A. (1993). A friend for life. *Thrust for Educational Leadership*, September, 44-46.

Mobley, D.W. (1993). Public education: Making it work. *Thrust for Educational Leadership*, September, 22-26.

Mulkey, J.R. (1993). Marketing your schools. *The Executive Educator*, July, 32-33.

Napolitan, J. (1987). Joseph Napolitan's greatest hints. *Campaigns and Elections*, May-June, 48-53.

Ogilvy, D. (1985). *Ogilvy on Advertising*. New York: Random House.

Osgood, C.E, Suci, G.J., & Tannenbaum, P.H. (1957). *The Measurement of Meaning*. Urbana, IL: University of Illinois Press.

Oxenfeldt, A.R. (1975). Developing a favorable price-quality image. *Journal of Retailing*, 50, 8-14.

Peters, T.J., & Austin, N. (1985). *A Passion for Excellence*. New York: Warner Books.

Preston, S. (1984). Children and the elderly in the U.S. *Scientific American*, December, 44-49.

Price, K. (1990). Yes at the polls. *Thrust for Educational Leadership*, September, 19-21.

Purvis, R.W. (1993). Improving school/community relations. *Thrust for Educational Leadership*, September, 47.

Quindlen, A. (1991). Citizen as consumer. *New York Times*, May 5, 17.

Rapp, S., & Collins T. (1987). *Maximarketing*. New York: McGraw-Hill Book Company.

Renihan, F.I., & Renihan, P.J. (1984). Effective schools, effective administration, and institutional image. *The Canadian Administrator*, 3, 1-6.

Ries, A., & Trout, J. (1986). *Positioning: The Battle for Your Mind*. New York: McGraw-Hill.

Robinson, S. (1991). Who needs to know what? *Thrust for Educational Leadership*, May-June, 18-20.

Rue, V.H. (1993). Bringing the community into your schools. *Thrust for Educational Leadership*, January, 24-26.

Sawyer, D.E., & Matsumoto, E.T. (1993). Low-effort high-return public relations programs. *Thrust for Educational Leadership*, September, 40-42.

Schlossberg, H. (1991). Marketers moving to make data bases actionable. *Marketing News*, February 18, 8-10.

Schreter, C. (1991). Older volunteers. *The American School Board Journal*, February, 35-36.

Senden, B. (1993). Success at the ballot box. *Thrust for Educational Leadership*, September, 37-39.

Shapiro, W. (1991). Tough choice. *Time*, September 16, 54-61.

Sharp, Deede, *in* Gilchrist, R.S. (1989). *Effective Schools: Three Case Studies of Excellence*. Bloomington, IN: National Educational Service.

Siegle, D. (1989). No news isn't good news: Effective media relations. *NASSP Bulletin*, January, 1-4.

Townley, A.J., & Schmieder, J.H. (1993). It's the children, stupid. *Thrust for Educational Leadership*, September, 32-36.

Tull, D.S., & Hawkins, D.I. (1984). *Marketing Research*. New York: Macmillan.

United Way of America (1990). Nine forces shaping America. Reprinted in *The Futurists*, July-August, 9-16.

Vercoe, J.D. (1971). Public relations in education. In *Proceedings of a Seminar on Public Relations*. Sydney, Australia: New South Wales Ministry of Education.

Walshak, H. (1991). An internal consensus can boost external success. *Marketing News*, June 10, 13.

Williams, J.K. (1993). Giving (and getting) good press. *Thrust for Educational Leadership*, September, 28-31.

Zemke, R. (1990). *The Service Edge*. New York: Dutton.

# DID YOU KNOW THAT WE NOW PROVIDE INSERVICE TRAINING?

The National Educational Service has a strong commitment to enhancing the lives of youth by producing top-quality, timely materials for the professionals who work with them. Our resource materials include books, videos, and professional development workshops in the following areas:

- Discipline with Dignity
- Reclaiming Youth at Risk
- Cooperative Learning
- Multicultural Awareness
- Cooperative Management
- Creating the New American School
- Parental Involvement

Our current mission focuses on celebrating diversity in the classroom and managing change in education.

# NEED MORE COPIES?

Need more copies of this book? Want your own copy? If so, you can order additional copies of *How Smart Schools Get and Keep Community Support* by using this form or by calling us at (800) 733-6786 (US only) or (812) 336-7700. Or you can order by FAX at (812) 336-7790.

We guarantee complete satisfaction with all of our materials. If you are not completely satisfied with any NES publication, you may return it to us within 30 days for a full refund.

|  | Quantity | Total Price |
|---|---|---|
| *How Smart Schools Get and Keep Community Support* ($18.95 each) | _____ | _____ |
| Shipping: Add $2.00 per copy (There is no shipping charge when you *include* payment with your order.) |  | _____ |
| Indiana residents add 5% sales tax |  | _____ |
| TOTAL |  | _____ |

❏ Check enclosed with order
❏ Please bill me (P.O. #_____)
❏ VISA or MasterCard
❏ Money Order

Account No._____ Exp. Date_____

Cardholder _____

Ship to:
Name_____ Title _____

Organization_____

Address _____

City_____ State_____ ZIP_____

Phone_____ FAX _____

MAIL TO:
National Educational Service
1610 West Third Street
P.O. Box 8
Bloomington, IN 47402